THIS BOOK
BELONGS TO

....

....

Thank you for Purchasing my book and taking the time to read it from front to back. I am always grateful when a reader chooses my work and I hope you enjoyed it!

With the vast selection available online, I am touched that you chose to be purchasing my work and take valuable time out of your life to read it. My hope is that you feel you made the right decision.

I very much would like to know what you thought of the book. Please take the time to write an honest and informative review on Amazon.com. Your experience and opinions will be of great benefit to me and those readers looking to make an informed choice.

With much thanks.

©COPYRIGHT 2024

The content contained within this book may not be reproduced, duplicated, or transmitted without direct written permission from the author or the publisher. Under no circumstances will any blame or legal responsibility be held against the publisher, or author, for any damages, reparation, or monetary loss due to the information contained within this book. Either directly or indirectly.

Legal Notice:
This book is copyright protected. This book is only for personal use. You cannot amend, distribute, sell, use, quote, or paraphrase any part, or the content within this book, without the consent of the author or publisher.

Disclaimer Notice:
Please note the information contained within this document is for educational and entertainment purposes only. All effort has been executed to present accurate, up-to-date, and reliable, complete information. No warranties of any kind are declared or implied. Readers acknowledge that the author is not engaging in the rendering of legal, financial, medical, or professional advice. The content within this book has been derived from various sources. Please consult a licensed professional before attempting any techniques outlined in this book. By reading this document, the reader agrees that under no circumstances is the author responsible for any losses, direct or indirect, which are incurred as a result of the use of the information contained within this document, including, but not limited to — errors, omissions, or inaccuracies.

Table of Contents

Introduction — 5
Chapter 1 : The Origin of Algo Trading — 8
Chapter 2 : All about Algos — 12
Chapter 3 : Trading Strategy Modelling Ideas — 24
Chapter 4 : Before Using Your Algos — 30
Chapter 5 : Testing Your Trading System — 41
Chapter 6 : Initial Analysis — 52
Chapter 7 : In - Depth Analysis — 61
Chapter 8 : Creating Your System — 67
Chapter 9 : Your Trade System Idea — 74
Chapter 10 : All about Data — 85
Chapter 11 : Diversifying Your Systems — 90
Chapter 12 : Money Management — 94
Chapter 13 : Documentation — 100
Conclusion — 104

Introduction

Imagine what it would be like to print money on autopilot. You go to bed, you wake up, and you're another million dollars richer — all without lifting a finger. Man, wouldn't that be a dream! All you've got is your trusty little robot or expert advisor whose job it is to make sure you wake up with more moolah in your pocket than you had the previous day.

Is it possible though? Not just to make millions, but also make millions on autopilot? Well, no doubt, if you're reading this book, then you know a fair bit about trading. You know you've got to either buy or sell stocks, or currency pairs, or whatever it is you choose to trade, and if it goes your way, then you've made a nice but of change. Right? How does it get better than that? How about the fact that all you need is the internet, and/or your cell phone?

Well, what if you could make all the money you need to, without even doing a thing? **Is that even possible?** Short answer, yes. We're talking about **algorithmic trading.** Spoiler alert! In case you missed the title, because the dog happened to the book cover before you could read it, that's what we're going to cover here.

Ever since the creation of trading robots and experts, the financial world has never been the same. Algorithmic trading is the future. And the future is here. Where algorithmic trading used to be a thing for just the big boys — you know, the hedge funds — now, it's for everyone. It's my job in this book to show you just how you too can benefit from algo trading!

You see, there is a reason that algorithmic trading has become so popular in today's world. It has so many advantages over manual trading — and I'm sure once you make the leap to algo trading, you won't even look back! Talk about speed, accuracy, and cost effectiveness. You can have all that and more with algo trading.

Todays' markets are far more volatile than they used to be. On account of this increased volatility, you're going to find algorithmic trading to be of benefit. That's because you'll be making your trading more efficient, by taking advantage of computing power. This means you'll get filled at better prices, and you'll have faster reactions to market events.

The days of accidentally entering trades is also going to be a thing of the past for you, once you choose algo trading over manual trading. There is no room for error, which means when you trade with algorithms, your capital will be safer than ever. All you need is the guidance, which I will provide you, to allow you create working strategy after working strategy, so you're always ahead of the curve.

You can say goodbye to having perfect trading setups ruined by your emotions. With algo trading, you'll be in a trade when you should be, and when it's time to get out, you'll be out.

Now I'm not even going to kid you — not even a little bit. This is going to be a lot of hard work. But it's going to be so worth it in the end. You'll see for yourself why the new way to trade is with algos. You'll learn how much better this style of trading is for you, than manual trading. You may have thought prior to now that this was the domain of only the big hedge funds and such. But this is not true! You, as a retail trader, can enjoy all the benefits of algorithmic trading as well, as you'll soon find out.

You're going to learn a whole lot. I'm going to make certain of that. Just do me a favor… Try to pay attention to everything you're reading here. This is serious business. Done right, algo trading is absolutely going to change the game for you, especially if you're a trader who constantly goes against the rules you've set up for taking trades, on account of those pesky human emotions named fear and greed. This could be the thing that turns it around for you.

This book is going to help you unlock the door to trading success. Now, all you have to do is walk right in. Let's begin.

Chapter 1: The Origin of Algo Trading

Ever wonder where the word 'algorithm' originated from? Well, there was this one Persian dude named Al Kwharizmi. He was no ordinary Persian dude. He was a mathematician, who lived in the area now known as present day Uzbekistan, around 820 AD. What's special about him? Well, he penned down a brilliant treatise. It was titled "Treatise on the Calculation with Arabic Numerals." I guess you could give him the credit for mathematics as we know it today. You know the word 'algebra.' Well, turns out he's the one who created that too, from the words 'al jabr', which means, "putting together."

Over the course of the 12th century, there were all sorts of translations of the word, and what used to be called 'algorism' became 'algorithm.' The beautiful thing about the idea behind algorithms is that it's multidisciplinary. It cuts across a lot of areas of life. It's also the one thing that makes your computers and everything they run on possible. That includes your cellphones too. I guess you could say algos rule the world. Yes, we're going to switch from calling them 'algorithms' to plain and simple 'algos.' It sounds cooler. Also it means I have that much less to type. Wins all round.

There are all sorts of algos, from the most basic to the most complex, for all sorts of functions. In this book, we're focusing on algos only as they relate to trading stocks.

Besides our Persian mathematician, there was some reference to algos back around 300 BC, in Euclid's Elements. It basically provided the best methods for calculating the Greatest Common Divisor (GCD) of two numbers. This is easily one of the granddaddies of formulas, which are still relevant in this day and age. You may know it as the Euclidean Algorithm. Man, would I love to be immortalized like that!

The First Algo Trade Ever

You're probably curious who the heck figured they could just set up an algorithm to trade on their behalf. Good question. I've got the scoop. We're going to go back in time to 19449, when the first ever hedge fund in the world was set up by a super clever dude named Alfred Winslow Jones. He basically made use of a really nifty strategy, keeping a balance between both long and short positions opened at the same time, with a ratio of 30:70 — 30 short, and 70 long. This was where quant finance began to take hold.

Borrowing Time

Now, on to the world of equities trading. When computers became even more popular and widely available early in the 1960s, some folks would play smart and shady at their day jobs. From their mainframe, they'd borrow some computer time, using it to analyze price action of various stocks over weeks and months, even. In fact, the first guy to have figured he could use a computer to analyze price action was Peter N. Haurlan. He was a rocket scientist (go figure). Using some of his incredible, rocket-science-y, technical skills, he would calculate stock data as relates to exponential moving averages. Eventually, he went on to publish the "Trade Levels Reports."

Block Trading

In the 1970s, block trading became a thing. Computers were well equipped at this point in time to handle block trades, which were trades worth about $1,000,000, or over 10,000 shares. Needless to say, as with all things novel, there was a lot of contention over this.

Pair Trading

You could say pair trading was really what kicked off algo trading. Who do we have to thank for this invention? Nunzio Tartaglia. To make this happen, Tartaglia put together a team of scientists across various disciplines, with Gerald Bamberger at the head, at Morgan Stanley. This was around 1980. Pair trading later became known as statistical arbitrage. You may have heard that referred to as 'stabarb,' in an attempt to make it sound hip, but quite frankly… Meh.

What happened next was pair trading became wildly successful. All of Wall Street was caught up in it. From the team Tartaglia created, other successful traders were created. They had figured out a way to really take advantage of computers, so they could do that much better than their colleagues. David Shaw? James Simons? You can actually trace their success back to Tartaglia's team.

Black Box

In no time, computers became beastly, with speeds and power never before imagined. They also became more mainstream. Naturally, the progress of algo trading moved in tandem with that of the computer. And, naturally, everyone wanted in on that action. Add in the creation of Direct Market Access for non-Exchange members, and algo trading just took off! Finally, the regular Jane and Joe could trade, through a broker. In no time flat, any trading desk worth its salt was trading with algos.

At Wall Street, the Buy side mutual funds with their vaults full of trillions of dollars, and the ever competitive Sell side brokerages realized they'd need people who actually knew how to run computers, if they were going to develop the Holy Grail of trading strategies. So they got the best minds from MIT, Harvard, and Stanford. No matter what these new hands on deck specialized in, they were all called 'quants.' Where once upon a time, the trading floor was packed full of colorful traders with even more colorful personalities, a new status quo has evolved. Technology was the new king, and it reigned supreme. So, now you know a little bit about the history of algorithmic trading, let's really sink our teeth into what algo trading is.

Chapter 2: All about Algos

Before we jump head first into the wonderful world of algos, let's clarify a few terms that are often mistaken for algorithmic trading, or misunderstood.

Quantitative Trading

Quantitative trading (or quant trading, for short) involves making use of advanced techniques based on statistics to make your decisions. These decisions may be made either manually, or automatically. Quantitative trading can be supplemented with algorithms, in order to completely remove the chance for human error. Quant trades may be high frequency, or low frequency. It all depends on the strategy.

High Frequency Trading (HFT)

This is a very special class of algo trading. One of the main characteristics of high frequency trading is the positions are held for very brief periods, during times of low-latency response, and with high volumes. The algos are programmed in such a way as to take advantage of opportunities which pop up ever so briefly — as brief as milliseconds, or even nanoseconds. While each trade has a relatively small margin, the incredible speed and volumes make up for that.

Algorithmic Trading

Algo trading is all about taking trades according to a predetermined set of rules. How is this different from manual trading? You already know the answer. In algo trading, you're not the one doing the trading. You've got your algo, which is set up to take trades on your behalf, according to the rules you've programmed. It's all systematic, leaving little room for human judgment or error. Computers are set up to give you valid trading signals, execute orders, and effectively manage portfolios.

A great way to further establish what algo trading is and isn't is to look at yet another popular trading style — discretionary trading. Here, the rules aren't exactly clear — if there are any at all. Where there **are** rules, they tend to be arbitrary, ever changing based on the whim of the trader. If you're a discretionary trader, then chances are you're used to always watching your screen. Chances are you also rely on your gut feelings a lot. The trouble with gut feelings is that there's really no way to measure them. Not yet anyway. So the only thing that could determine your success with 'gut feelings' would be your trading statement. Now, I'm not trying to say there is no successful discretionary trader out there. I'm just saying the entire process of learning to trade this way can take forever. It takes its toll not just on your mind, but even your bank account.

Algos: Not Just for HFTs

There's the impression that algo trading is only ever done by the big boys. The sharks. The High Frequency Trading (HFT) firms, who have access to state of the art technology and all the speed they need to get their orders in before you click buy or sell with your puny little mouse. They've got a whole crew of experts with more PhDs than you could ever hope to have under your belt, all in the process of creating and tweaking algos which take advantage of every single move in price, no matter how small. How can you even compete with that? If you're a scalper, then you should know these are the guys who make it hard for you to scalp just a tick or two for profit. You could try, but it's more than likely you'll always be on the losing side.

Well, I've got news for you. You can be an algo trader. You don't have to have a whole room full of computers from the future to do this. In fact, there's no need to try to recreate precisely what the algo traders at HFTs do. Where would you get the time and money to do that anyway? Or the expertise? Well the good news is you don't need all that. You, as a retail trader, a small fish in the big bad sea of sharks, can trade with algos with the best of them.

Rather than scalp your account balance into the red, did you know you could actually beat the HFTs at their own game by using algo trading for longer trades? I'm talking about day trading, swing trading, and position trading. You've probably tried this before, but with algos, you have an even better edge. You can get all the benefits without the bruises. I think that's a win.

Backtesting Algos

In a nutshell, algo trading follows the rules, one hundred percent. There's no room for discretion. There's no point where you look at a candlestick and think, "Hmm, I don't know, maybe I really shouldn't be short there. Also, Trump just tweeted **again.** No telling what will happen next." The algo you've programmed will execute. And it will do so flawlessly. You can program your algo into whatever trading software you use, and it will take trades based on the conditions you've set for it.

One of the awesome things about algo trading is that you can backtest it. Backtesting is basically making use of historical data from price action, to see how well your strategy — in this case, your algo — would have performed over time. Yes, in trading, we always say that past results are not indicative of future performance. The markets can and do change from time to time. But the great thing about backtesting your algo is it shows you whether or not what you've created is indeed profitable, without you having to risk real money with forward testing live trades.

The great thing about being able to backtest your algos, is that since there is very little room for any arbitrary trades, it paints a more accurate picture that you'd get from backtesting a discretionary strategy. This is because the sequence of steps you program into your algo remain constant, and as you already know, "garbage in, garbage out."

Algos in Action

Algos follow rules, or parameters, which you set. Now, there are some algos, which are actually adaptive in nature, in that the rules are set up to change depending on the market condition, and the contingency parameters you set up.

If you're going to make money from algo trading, then your algos need to be based on very, very solid strategy — which means setting up the right parameters. This is going to be the deciding factor on whether or not you make money trading stocks in the long run.

So how exactly do algos work? Algos run on a very precise set of rules, which are dependent on the price of the stock, the time of day, the amount, and a number of other mathematical models.

Let's take a very simplistic example. You could set it up so your algo purchases 100 shares of GOOGL (that's the ticker symbol for Alphabet Inc., the mad geniuses behind Google) each time it's 14 period exponential moving average crosses the 50 period moving average bullish. You could also set it up so when the 14 period exponential moving average or EMA crosses the 50 period EMA downward or bearish, sell trades are executed.

(In case you're wondering what a moving average is, it's basically a measurement of the average of the movement of price over a period of time - which is determined by you, the trader. There are different sorts of moving averages. The exponential places the most relevance on the most recent price action.)

Based on these parameters you have set up, your algo will help you monitor the price of the stock(s) you're trading, and either go long (buy) or go short (sell) when the right conditions line up. You won't have to stick your butt to the chair and glue your eyes on the screen in the name of monitoring your trades. This is the algos job.

Benefits of Trading with Algos

When you trade with algos, what you'll notice is your trades are executed with precision. You get filled at the best, most accurate prices, down to the tick. This is rarely the case with discretionary trading — unless you somehow have your trading platform wired directly to your brain or something. In addition to getting in at the best prices, you also are not likely to have your orders unfilled.

Algos help you make sure your trades are correctly timed, so you don't have to deal with the messiness of drawdown — at least, you won't need to deal with more drawdown than your strategy allows for. Also, because of the precision of entries and timing, you'll find that you have to deal with less transaction costs, from your spread, among other factors.

It's possible to monitor the multiple stocks in the market, and monitor each one across different time frames, using algorithms. This means you're less likely to experience the overwhelming feeling that can come from having to process so much information, which leads to analysis paralysis, and causes you to enter a few ticks too late.

When you're an algo trader, you never have to worry about errors when trading. At least, not as much as the manual, discretionary traders do. The algos follow rules to the letter, so there's no way it's going to trigger a buy when you wanted it to trigger a sell.

What other benefits can you get from algo trading? You can easily backtest using past data as well as real time data, so you can determine whether or not your strategy is actually worth its salt.

The best part? The complete elimination of errors due to human emotion or psychology. Your algos don't care that they haven't had lunch, or that they just had a huge argument with their spouses. They're going to execute just as flawlessly as they always have. If that isn't a thing of beauty, then I don't know what is.

Algo Trading Systems

Trading systems are also known as 'trading strategies.' They're basically a set of conditions and rules, which govern how you enter and exit your trades — both long and short.

When you're coming up with a strategy, you basically need to observe and exploit a set of market conditions that will both give you profits, and reduce your trading costs at the same time. Yes, you do need to pay attention to trading costs as well, because the fact of the matter is they can and do eat into your profits, if your strategy is not sound enough. That said, let's talk about a few possible strategies for trading stocks based on algos.

Trend Following Strategies

Trend following strategies are some of the most common strategies for trading stocks with algos. No surprise there. Trend following strategies usually incorporate moving averages, breakouts, price action at significant levels or round figures, among other indicators. The great thing about trend following strategies is how simple they are. You don't need to call tops and bottoms. You don't need to channel the ghost of Nostradamus to figure out where price is going to go next. All you need to do with strategies like this is simply figure out the current trend, and then hop on it, until it goes the other way. One of the most popular trend following strategies involves the use of the 50-period moving average and the 200-period moving average.

Range Trading Strategies

Also known as 'mean reversion trading,' range trading strategies are a different animal than trend trading. Where with trend trading you buy the dip, and sell the rally in line with a given trend, with range trading, you'll be selling into upward movements, and buying into downward movements. This isn't quite the same thing, because with range trading, the assumption is that the value of the stock is only ever temporary, and it will always return to the mean or average, sooner or later. So an algorithm, which follows a mean reversion strategy, takes trades as soon as price moves in and out of its current range. Strategies like this would be extremely useful in a sideways market, where the price chops with no particular direction, but within a defined range.

Market Making

If you're not so new to trading, then you've probably heard of 'market makers.' A market maker's job is to provide liquidity to those securities, which are not traded all that often on the stock exchange. The market maker is in the unique position of controlling the demand and supply of securities.

For example, the market maker may buy 1,000 shares of NIKE (NKE) for $200 each. This is the ask price. Then the market maker turns around and sells those shares to a willing buyer at $200.10. $.10 may seem like quite a small bit of profit, but understand that the market maker trades millions and millions of shares each day. As a result of them 'making the market,' they're able to pocket quite an impressive amount of profits, taking care of the risks completely.

Mathematical Trading Strategies

These follow solid rules based on tried and true mathematical models. For example, you have trading strategies based off of the delta-neural, and you have the Murrey Math trading strategy, among other strategies. The delta neural are structured in such a way that the positions you trade are going to remain relatively unaffected by minute movements in the price of the stock. These strategies help you make profits by exploiting time and volatility, and also are great for hedging — which is how your account stays protected through all the fluctuations in price.

Time Weighted Average Price Strategies

These are based on time. Your large orders are essentially split up into smaller ones, according to predetermined rules based off of very precise time slots. All orders are filled as close as possible to the mean price of the stock, between the beginning and ending times. This way, the market's impact on the positions and your overall account balance is minimized.

Arbitrage Trading

Arbitrage trading involves dual-listed stocks. You sell the stock at a much higher price in one market, while buying it for less in another market. The difference in prices between both stocks will serve as your profit, which is risk free. This is arbitrage. With this strategy, your algo is programmed to spot the differences in price between the stocks you're monitoring, and then it places the trades accordingly, letting you reap the profits.

Black Lance

Sounds super cool, doesn't it? Like some sort of weapon in an RPG. The algos based off this strategy are created with one sole purpose: to discover liquidity in 'dark pools.' Almost sounds like we're discussing something cooler than trading, doesn't it? The way it discovers and dredges up the liquidity from these dark depths is by 'pinging' various venues, and then running an analysis on the responses it receives.

Iceberg

With this strategy, the point is to keep large orders hidden from traders and other participants in the market, so as to avoid them getting in ahead of you. It also helps reduce the costs that can be accrues as a result of the market's movement, when working on accumulating a large position on your preferred stock. Rather than jump in at one go with a heavy order, your order is split up into smaller, less suspicious fragments, and then placed at random prices. There's also another version of the iceberg which makes use of limit orders, and is generally for trades which take place over a longer period of time than usual.

Of course, algos that employ the iceberg strategy are mainly used by the big sharks, or institutions with a lot of stock they need to move around. When using the iceberg strategy, it's more important to stay anonymous, than to make profits — because the anonymity almost always guarantees returns, anyway.

The Peg

Algos based on this strategy place limit orders, keeping the fraction of the whole order random. Then they follow the market, just like a trailing order does.

Volume Weighted Average Price Strategies

These are among the oldest and most popular of algo trading strategies, so we're going to dive in a bit deeper here. They make use of the unique volume profiles of the stocks you trade to split up your larger orders, letting go of a set amount of your orders to the market. In other words, depending on just how liquid the stock is, algos based off of this strategy make use of both past data and real time volume data, using them as conditions based upon which large orders will be sliced into bits, over a time period. It's usually used on orders that last longer than average.

Another upside to using the VWAP strategy is not only does it help reduce the effect of the markets on your orders, but it also keeps the size of your order undetectable by other participants in the market. On account of the characteristics of the market during the earlier and later parts of the trading sessions, there will be even more volume traded during these times, in order to prevent any undesirable effects on price.

In calculating VWAP, the following formula applies:
$$P_{vwap} = (P * V)/V$$

Where
P_{vwap} = volume weighted average price
P = price of each trade
V = volume of each trade

Serial Algos

Serial algos contain a set of instructions, which are implemented serially. In other words, the instructions are set up to execute one after the other. The algos will definitely have logic control implemented to avoid them developing a mind of their own and blowing through your account.

Parallel Algos

These are based off of strategies, which implement several instructions at the same time.

Recursive Algos

Any strategy using recursive algos is basically set up so that they 'call' each other for as many times as is required, until the conditions you've set have been met.

Iterative Algos

These algos handle order executions based on conditions like, 'if… then,' 'do while,' 'for… next.' They will usually have programmable parameters and values, which can be tweaked to make better decisions.

Pair Trading Strategy

This strategy was what gave algo trading a shove into the limelight. I'll describe this as simply as possible.

Over the years, there has been quite an increase in volatility, and also in the levels of most stocks. The swings in the market have become even more dramatic — and this isn't just in reference to the financial meltdown of 2008. Because of this, the prospect of a market neutral trading — one that still produces desirable results despite what the market of doing — has become even more attractive, and vital.

Pair trading is about as market neutral as it gets. This is not a strategy that is rocked by market direction. It is strictly based on the correlative and anti-correlative behavior of stocks.

Tartaglia had discovered that there were particular stocks — more often than not in the same industries and sectors — tended to demonstrate correlation in price action. He hypothesized that if there were any changes to the movement of both stocks, they would both revert to the mean over a period of time. His hypothesis was proven correct — and Wall Street went on to make a killing off it, for the next two decades.

So what's pair trading, in a nutshell? Let's take a look at two correlated stocks. Say one begins an uptrend, while the other begins a downtrend. What you do in this scenario is short the stock that's doing well, and go long on the stock that's performing poorly. The theory is eventually, both stocks will revert to the mean, and in the process, you will have netted profits on both trades.

One of the best things about pair trading is its market neutrality. So if something goes belly up, you're not affected, because with your buy and sell positions, you're effectively hedged. Your positions are immune to news, someone accidentally putting in too many orders at once, or a certain president tweeting something controversial. However, I should point out the possibility for risk, when one of the stocks is going through liquidity crises, and you are unable to close out your position.

If you're going to use the pair trading strategy, then you'll need to find two stocks which have shown correlation with each other over a period of time — said period of time being our preferred lookback period. We program the algo so it can spot when there's a difference in the status quo between both stocks, and once price on both stocks has deviated to the programmed limit, it swiftly executes trades. The algo will then monitor the price still, sometimes over days, weeks even, and once the stocks have shown their back to being correlated, both trades will be closed.

There are many other strategies, which can be implemented with algos to net you profits. These are just a handful of them.

To create a profitable strategy, you'll need a lot of research, which is usually carried out by the 'quants,' as they are called in the world of algo trading. These are basically the mad geniuses that come up with valid strategies, using statistical and mathematical models, so they can create a strategy that generates profits regardless of market conditions.

Chapter 3: Trading Strategy Modelling Ideas

Strategy Paradigms

We're going to jump right in to discussing the paradigms, which apply to algorithmic trading strategies — specifically statistical arbitrage, market making, momentum, and machine learning based strategies.

Market Making Model

As we mentioned before, when it comes to market making, the primary goal is to create liquidity in stocks which are rarely traded on the exchanges. When we take stock of just how much liquidity there is, we need to factor in the current spread — being the difference between the bid and the ask prices — as well as the volume of trades.

The way a trading algorithm based off of a market making strategy would make money is by pocketing the difference between the bid and the ask. Let's take a simple example. We'll refer to the market maker as MM.

So, MM, being a liquidity provider, is in the unique position to quote prices on both the buy side and the sell side of a certain set of stocks. He plans to make some money from the difference between the bid and the ask, or the spread, if you will. So he takes on the risk of being in possession of the stocks.

Once he gets a buy order, he is quick to sell from what he already has, at a much higher price than he got the asset for. In a matter of seconds, MM decides to offset that deal, by being a buyer again. This time, when he buys, he buys from a seller at a much lower price, and then turns around and repeats the process again.

One thing to keep in mind is that in stocks with very low liquidity, the spreads are often higher. This means MM is going to take on a lot more risk, as a result of the lack of interested investors in that particular stock. On the flip side, it also means his gains will be even higher than the risk. MM is generous, ever willing to take both buys and sells at the prices he quotes. As a matter of fact, a lot of high frequency trading really is just market making in disguise, in its most passive form. When is the strategy of market making most likely to yield profit? For however long this model correctly predicts future price action.

Let's discuss briefly about the modelling ideas based on market making. First of all, the trade volume, as well as the spread, may both be modeled together, in order to determine the cost curve of liquidity. This liquidity cost curve is basically the fee it will cost the one who takes on the liquidity. In the event that this 'liquidity taker' places orders at the best possible bid and ask, then to calculate the fee, the spread must be multiplied by the volume of the trade. Note that whenever the traders **do** go a bit beyond the spread and take on more volume, then the liquidity fee will depend heavily on the volume.

It's not so easy to model trade volume. This is because it largely depends on the strategy by which the liquidity taker executes their trades. So what the goal is here, is to come up with a working model for trade volumes, which is completely in line with the unique dynamics of price action. So when it comes to market making models, you have one of the following:

- A model, which has inventory risk as its sole focus. The foundation here would be the chosen inventory price and position, which are dictated by the risk appetite.
- A model with a focus on adverse selection. Here, there is a clear distinction made between trades, which are informed and based on solid parameters, as well as trades, which are simply noise. The difference here is when it comes to 'noisy trades,' there really isn't a particular bias on where the market is

headed, but when it comes to informed trades, there is a clear view on current and future price action. If the liquidity taker is intent on making a profit in the short term, then this will be accomplished by means of a statistical edge. For the longer term trades, however, the goal is to keep transaction costs to a minimum, as much as possible. Strategies, which are designed to work over the longer term, in conjunction with liquidity shortage, could be viewed as nothing more than noise, as far as the shorter term strategies are concerned.

Statistical Arbitrage Model

Where the marking maker's model seeks to make a profit from the difference between the bid and the ask prices, statistical arbitrage is the strategy which is used to make a profit from the stocks deemed statistically mispriced.

In stabarb, the risk is fanned out across trades numbering from a thousand to a million, and held for really short periods of time, with a view to making gains by the law of large numbers. As we've already covered before, this strategy depends hugely on the concept of mean reversion.

In order to understand the modelling ideas for statistical arbitrage, let's take a closer look at pair trading, which is but one of the strategies possible under the stabarb category.

With pair trading, there are certain stocks, which over time have shown the likelihood of moving in tandem with each other. They've shown similar fundamentals. So the model here is firmly founded on the hypothesis that any deviations from this norm will eventually be corrected, and equilibrium will be restored.

The model holds that in order to take advantage of the deviations and restoration of balance, the outperforming stock is shorted, while the underperforming stock is bought. This strategy is beta neutral, on account of positions being hedged against adverse market conditions. The total risk of each position would be completely based on how much capital you invest in each stock, and how sensitive those stocks are to sudden whipsaws.

Momentum Models

With this algo trading strategy, the goal is to enter positions for the short term in stocks, which are showing clear signs of a trend up, or down, and to hold the position until there is a clear sign of reversal. Where a strategy like value investing is long term, and seeks to take advantage of mean reversion, momentum investing takes advantage of the time and price action in the period before reversion to the mean takes place.

For momentum trading, it's all about systematically going after performance. It involves taking advantage of other traders who are also going after performance, based off of decisions skewed by emotions. Throughout the course of history, there are only ever two reasons for strategies, which work: the strategy is based off of behavioral conditions, or the inherent risk in the strategy is adequately compensated for.

Momentum works on account of a very, very long list of biases and emotion driven mistakes on the part of investors. Capitalizing on these is no mean feat though, because as you've probably noticed when you look through your charts, there's no such thing as a trend that lasts forever. Price runs its course when it hits significant levels and creates those dreaded M and W patterns, which we know most likely, will signal the end of the trend! At this point, the trend is **not** your friend,

To really take advantage of momentum, the 'momo trader' — what momentum based traders are called — will need to take advantage of high volatility, more than traders using other strategies. They also need to jump into their long and short positions at the correct time, using sound risk management techniques. The momo trader's best friend is a stop loss. Investing in stocks this way will require constant monitoring, and to be safe, it would be best to diversify trades, in case of crashes.

What are the modelling ideas behind the momo trade? First, the trader needs to be able to detect the current trend. If you've been trading a while — most likely manually — then you know the best way to figure out the trend is to watch for stocks which have been going up — or down — for a long period of time, be it days, weeks, or even months in a row. You can do this by pinpointing the stocks, which trade within at least 10% of their high over the last 52 weeks. You could also observe the percentage price change over the past 12 weeks, or even 24 weeks. If you're looking for a much shorter trend, then all you need to do is reduce the time frame you're considering.

When we go back a little over a decade to 2008, there was some buzz about how the oil and energy sector was one of the top sectors — despite the collapse it was suffering. To really understand the price action of stocks, you would do well to take a look at earnings. Any strategy which is founded on historical returns (such as momo strategies) or earnings surprise (earnings momo strategies) are set up to take advantage of times when the market doesn't quite react to certain fundamentals or news. Where the earnings momo trader makes her profit from under-reaction to news concerning short term earnings, the price momo trader makes profits from the market's inability to respond fast enough to much broader, more long-term information.

Machine Learning Models

When it comes to trading based on machine learning trading, the algos have to make short term predictions of the range of price action at key 'confidence intervals.' The best part about using AI is while humans are responsible for developing said AI, the AI goes on to further work on making itself better and better over time. In other words, the machine learns. While there are a large number of funds, which thrive on computer based models, which have been created by wants and data scientists, these are usually static. They never change along with the market. However, machine learning models are dynamic, and are able to process a large amount of data at incredible speeds, then analyze them, and subsequently make adjustments for the better based off of their analysis.

Let's talk a bit on the modelling idea behind machine learning models. We're specifically going to take a closer look at a certain sort of machine learning, which is known as 'Bayesian networks.' Bayesian networks are used to determine market trends in advance. They do this using only a couple of machines. An AI which has evolutionary computation and deep learning programmed into it can be run with hundreds of machines — sometimes even thousands. The AI has the ability to test historical performances of a large, randomized set of stock traders, and then implement the most profitable styles of trading to replicate the results. Once created, this AI trader needs no external input, and can run fully automated.

Chapter 4: Before Using Your Algos

The whole point behind trading, whether you're using algos or not, is to make profits. So how exactly can you achieve this, using algos? One key thing to keep in mind is you want to make profit from each trade. As often as possible, of course.

The individual trader is small fry in a world of whales, sharks, and octopi with all their grubby, greedy legs. Rarely do you see an individual trader with positions of more than 1,000 to 2,500 shares at one go. As far as the big kahunas go, individual traders barely make a dent in price action. They're nothing but noise.

But don't let all that get to you. The good thing is, as a solitary trader, you don't have to be overly worried about liquidity. All you need to do is choose stocks that are liquid more often than not. You definitely do not want to trade any stocks, which are barely traded — anything less than 500,000 shares for each session is a no-no.

Manual Trading

Before you begin trading with your algos, it's important that you trade the strategy behind them manually. Yes, the whole point behind trading algos is to not have to interfere with your trades, but the truth is manual trading — at least beforehand — is the best way to actually get a feel for what it's like trading stocks with your algo.

When you trade manually, you'll be able to pick out what works and what doesn't work. This is only going to be in the beginning of your journey with algo trading. Once you have had more practice with creating your own trading systems, then you can leave behind manual trading for good. That's a guarantee.

Trading Simulators

You want to practice your strategy with a good simulator. One you can use intuitively. There are several good ones available. Thinkorswim by TD Ameritrade and Bear Bull Traders simulator are examples of good ones.

It's important for you to get familiar with whatever trading simulator you decide to go with. That is because you need everything you do with the simulator to be second nature. You also want to avoid the mistakes of curve fitting, over optimizing, or accidentally entering the wrong parameters in your strategy testing process. Trust me when I say this can be a very costly mistake — one I'm not ashamed to say I've made before, because I learned from it. You don't have to repeat the same mistakes I did.

So take your time with your trading simulator. If you want to also learn programming, then commit to learning the language for the simulator as well. In the long run, you'll be glad you did. This is because it will save you from spending so much money hiring experts. Nothing wrong with that, but you should keep in mind that you'll need to hire expert coders over and over again, and like it or not, that's also a part of your trading costs.

Setting Up Your Parameters

When programming your algos, you need to set up your parameters as carefully as possible. By parameters, I'm referring to the constants among all the values in the formula of your algo. This is the only way to ensure good **and** accurate results. For instance, you may need to adjust the lookback period every now and then, depending on any changes you encounter in your preferred stocks' price action. You want to make this a daily practice, if you can. Historical data from at most five sessions is more than enough.

Know Thy Algo

If you're going to use an algo, then you want to know it inside out, top down. You need to understand all the formulae, and all the bits and pieces that go into creating your algo. In other words, you must look under the hood, and perform a SWOT analysis of your algo. This will help you in the long run to be free from errors as a result of emotions of uncertainty, which might cause you to tweak trades or settings you really should leave alone.

When you know your algo inside and out, then you'll find yourself less swayed by the all-too-natural emotions, which come to play with trading. You come to rely less on the not-so-reliable traits of 'gut feeling.' and simply place your trust in the well thought-out, well-crafted formula behind your algo.

Another way to keep your algos straight is to document everything related to them that is relevant to developing your strategy. Don't just keep the facts in your head. I don't care if your memory is that good. Trust me when I say it is way better to write it down.

As a true algo trader, you're going to work on hundreds and hundreds of systems. How are you going to keep all that straight without actually taking notes? You need to know how each algo works, and why it does what it does. You need to remember what you were thinking when you created each algo. What I'm saying, in a nutshell, is you can never overestimate the importance of proper documentation.

Trade Fit, or Not At All

When trading, do not underestimate the importance of your physical and mental wellbeing. This doesn't just apply to manual trading, but to algo trading as well. You don't want to let your algos run the shop when you're upset or unwell. Make sure you're in top shape, so you can handle whatever anomalies might arise as you trade, if any do come up.

Trust Thy Algo

There can be no room for doubt here. You cannot afford any second guessing. Second guessing leads to tweaking, and this can lead to inaccurate results. What once may have been a profitable algo can then become unprofitable, because you decide to change this and fix that, or to close or open trades where you really shouldn't have. This is not the time to be a micromanager. All that does is drain you emotionally and mentally — and this is just contrary to the whole point of trading algos to begin with. We can do without emotions in trading. This will help us see the bigger picture better. So stop tinkering, and trust the algo! At least, until it proves itself untrustworthy.

The Goal is Mastery

Think of algo trading as a skill. Like all skills you acquire over time, you need consistent practice. If you're going to hone your abilities as an algo trader, then you need to do your best and focus on getting better. There will never be perfection. But you can keep striving for it. This is the correct attitude to assume.

You'll need lots of patience, and lots of practice, if you intend to get the results you desire. So make sure you do have time for this. There can be nothing and no one else during your set times for mastering stocks with algo trading. This means you need to check out various trading stations or platforms, to see which ones work best for you. Then you need to get familiar with the controls. Get the mechanics down pat. The goal is to become mechanical when operating your Order Management System. You want to automatically know the shortcut keys to opening trades, closing them, trailing them. Know everything inside out. This takes time. However long it takes, keep at it, until it all becomes automatic to you.

Elements of Algo Trading

These are the basics:

Data is King

Data is your best friend. Past data, and real time data. It's imperative that you are able to access data for all the sessions you intend to trade in. Where exactly do you get this data to begin with? We're going to take a look at the exchange for an emerging market.

It's the NSE, which is responsible for providing market quotes and data to various market segments such as the Capital Market Segment, and the Wholesale Debt Market Segment. The NSE also provides market quotes to the Currency Derivative Market Segment, Securities Lending & Borrowing Market as well as the Futures and Options Segment, and even Corporate Data.

DotEx International Ltd, a subsidiary of NSE, is responsible for providing the quotes. It sends out data in real time to all the information agencies. There are 5 different kinds of data products provided by the NSE, as listed above. There are also 4 levels of data provided. Let's get into it.

Level 1 data gives the Best Bid and Best ASk, as well as the Bid Size and Ask Size.

Level 2 data gives market depth data of up to 5 best bid and bet ask prices.

Level 3 data gives market depth data of about 20 best bid and ask prices.

Tick-by-tick data basically contains every single order or change in orders.

As a new trader, you only need level 1 data for you to analyze the charts, and come up with strategies to help you make your decisions when trading. Any other sort of data is mostly used by the more experienced traders, and high frequency trading institutions and firms.

Data Vendors

NSE is responsible for providing data to the data vendors, who have been authorized to redistribute this data to trading firms, brokerages, and retail traders as well. A few data vendors for the American markets include Bloomberg, CQG, Cbonds, Dealogic, Fidessa, and FactSet, to name a few.

While some data vendors only provide the data feed, others also give charting platforms as well as analytics and options for creating customized watch lists, developing strategies, tracking various markets, generating long and short signals, and so much more. As a trader, you can simply connect to the platform with your broker's platform. You do this through a bridge. This is how your orders are executed. As with most data vendors, you'll find their broker partners listed on their web pages, and you'll also see what charting platforms are most compatible with their data feed.

Let's take a close look at one of the world's leading data vendors, eSignal. No, this is not an endorsement; this is purely to help you understand how data vendors work. eSignal offers three major products: **Signature**, **Classic**, and **Elite**.

The most popular of the three products happens to be **Signature.** Signature offers advanced charting with highly customizable studies or indicators, real-time data streaming, stocks, futures, forex and options, backtesting, historical data for 1 year intra-day, the ability to download data using Qlink or RTD, news, commentary, and research. The Qlink service allows you to download streaming, real-time data into Excel worksheets, allowing you to analyze and build your strategies, and then to execute them using Excel API.

Charting Platforms Are Necessary

Every true trader needs a charting platform. You do, if you're going to make money. It's imperative that you get familiar with the different charting platforms available, as well as expose yourself to as many charting techniques as you can, so you can find the right one for you to make profits from the stock market. If you're wondering which charting platforms to go for, a few of the more popular ones are MetaStock, AmiBroker, NinjaTrader, TradeStation, cTrader, and eSignal. Not an exhaustive list, but these are good ones to try.

What features do you get with most charting platforms? You get scanning (real-time), technical indicators, backtesting, expert advisors, scripts, automatic trades, fundamentals, news services, forecasts, level 2 data, and so on. It all varies from platform to platform. You need to choose one which best suits your trading style, taking into consideration the features of the platform, as well as the pricing. Let's take a quick look at MetaStock, for example.

MetaStock is quite popular. It has loads of features and solutions for those who trade real-time, those who trade end of day, and those who trade the Forex markets. You have such features as DataLink, MetaStock daily charts, MetaStock Xenith, MetaStock Real Time, as well as various third-party add-ons, to make for a well-rounded trading experience.

Programming Is Necessary

When trading with algos, it invariably involves the process of creating and coding strategies, which are based on the in-depth analysis of past data and real-time data provided by the data vendors. You need to keep in mind that some of the previously mentioned charting platforms have their own special languages for scripting, which you can use to code your algos and backtest your strategies directly on the platforms as well.

Today, Python is one of the most widely used and accepted programming languages for algo traders all around the world. We have Van Rossum to thank for that, as he created this program in order to appeal to C hackers and Unix hackers alike.

Almost universally, algo traders make use of languages like Java, Matlab, and Python for trading on whatever their preferred trading platform is. There are lots of third party analytical packages employed in these languages — to the tune of hundreds, even. These packages assist greatly when developing momentum, mean reversion, scalping, and sentimental strategies, as well as those strategies, which involve machine learning algorithms. Then the traders make use of 'external wrappers', which help execute the codes onto their trading platform.

If you're going to be an algo trader — a successful one, at that — then you definitely need to have a solid foundation in programming. You've got to learn the basics of programming, and also figure out how to create and program your own strategies for various market conditions with these programming languages.

Brokers Matter

When trading, you've absolutely got to choose the right broker for you. What are some of the things you need to consider when choosing a broker? First of all, they need to be licensed. You want to know that you can trust your broker with your money, so making sure they are licensed and registered with the relevant bodies is one way to go about that.

Next, you want to be certain that their trading platform is fast, and reliable. Fortunately, most brokers offer demo accounts, so you can try out their platform before you put your real cash on the line.

Another thing to consider is what trading segments are offered by the broker. If the segment you intend to trade is not offered, then it goes without saying that's not the broker you want to choose.

Other things to consider is what leverage they offer. You also need to think about the margin requirements of the broker you're choosing. Both leverage and margin are important, because you want to be sure neither will adversely affect your trading strategy. Same goes for commissions as well. If you're a scalper, commissions can easily eat into your profits, so be careful of that.

You also need to know whether your charting platform is compatible with your broker. If they are not, then you either need to master the platforms offered by the broker, or move on to another that does work with your platform of choice.

Finally, you need to think about the gateway APIs the broker offers you. In the event that your PC freezes up, or crashes, you need to know you've got a good API that will still execute your stop and limit orders, even then. Otherwise you might have the sort that simply leaves your orders hosted on your computer, rather than on the broker's server. Brokers will usually list the APIs they have available on their web pages. Some brokers offer you platforms that are actually a bunch of simple HTTP APIs constructed on their online, web-based trading platforms. These exchange approved platforms allow you as a trader to access data like your funds, your profile, current orders, limit orders, order history, live quotes, positions, and so on. You can also execute orders and manage them as well, using your preferred programming language — be it Java, C#, excel VBAs, or Python.

A Working System

At this point, it should be pretty clear to you what you'll be working with, as an algo trader. You'll need charting platforms, the right broker terminal, a news feed, good programming tools, a good data stream, and a bunch of other stuff. You'll need to work with a bunch of different applications, know how to handle a huge amount of data for your backtesting, do your forward tests, and do a bunch of different things **at the same time** while trading live. That said, it's important that you have the right computer system to handle all of this and more without any hiccups. The last thing you need is to have the blue screen of death show up right before you could put a stop loss on your newly opened position!

The whole point behind trading algorithmically, is to avoid the entire hassle that comes with being overly involved emotionally with your trades. It's to get your trading automated. How do you automate trading without a proper machine? You need something better than a laptop. Though some traders are comfortable and quite successful trading from laptops (and even their cellphones!) you're just starting out. You should get a proper computer system. A high-end one, with multiple monitors.

Your chosen system needs to have a high RAM, a fast processor, and quality graphics cards. The motherboard needs to be trustworthy, and you need to have as much storage space as you can. If you're going to be doing this and making money off of it, then you definitely need the right system. So do some research. Talk with people who are knowledgeable about computers, so you get the best kind.

These are the minimum requirements your computer should have, if you're going to trade stocks with algos:

Operating System:
    Windows — Windows Vista, Windows 7, Windows 8, Windows 8.1, Windows 10.
    Mac — Mac (v 10.7), Mac (v 10.8), Mac (v 10.9), Mac (v 10.10), Mac (v 10.11), Mac (v 10.12), Mac (v 10.13)

RAM: 3GB DDR3
Processor: Intel Core i5, 2.40 GHz

Software you'll most likely find useful include R and RStudio, Microsoft Excel, and Anaconda (Python) - 2.7, and 3.6.

Chapter 5: Testing Your Trading System

In order to design your own trading system, you absolutely need to learn how to test a system's performance metrics. It may seem super easy and straightforward, but I assure you this is no mean feat. So you understand what I'm trying to say, let's look at an example.

Let's assume you have an equity curve for a stock trading system — one generated by testing a strategy. (You can find these available on the net for free; any software worth its salt will give you all sorts of metrics to examine). When you take a look at the equity curve for the strategy you just tested, as well as other reports on performance, you might find yourself with more questions than you began with.

You start to wonder. What do these results mean? Are they really good, or bad? Are they even believable to begin with? Do they actually have any value in predicting real time results with this strategy? How exactly can I weed out what doesn't work from what does?

If It's Too Good to Be True...

Whenever you take a look at reports equity curves and such, it's best to adhere to that old wise saying. You know the one. "If it's too good to be true, it probably is." Why do I say this? This is because any trader who has been at this long enough already knows "past results are not indicative of future performance."

In other words, you may have tested it, and your backtest may have revealed an equity curve so steep only Spiderman could climb without falling, but the truth is, the better the test results are (tests based on past price action, that is) the more likely your strategy will suck in the future.

Now, this is not always the case, obviously. There are a few exceptions here and there. The more you spend time creating your own trading strategies, the easier it is to discover these rule breaking, profitable strategies.

This begs the question, why do past results look so good if they're only going to end up being terribly, irredeemably bad? There's a little something known as the 'survivorship bias.' What this means is most unscrupulous vendors will only ever show the good results of trading systems historically tested. Think about it. What vendor in their right mind would want to sell you a system with historical results, which are just plain bad for your account's health? Would you trade a system with such utterly crappy results? Of course you wouldn't. So it only makes sense to leave out the bad results, and only display the food.

A Different Scenario

Another possibility is that the test results based off of past price action are actually valid and true. It's possible the developer has indeed discovered an actually edge. The thing to keep in mind though, is that it's quite possible for this edge to become duller and duller as time goes on. This can happen either because other people stumble upon this edge, or the market suddenly begins to act differently, or for any other reason under the trading sun, really.

What happens with such a system is it inevitably does its own mean reversion act — meaning, at best, what you'll have is a strategy which lets you breakeven — and that's assuming you're not factoring in the commissions and other trading costs which can and do accrue per trade.

Testing Method Plays a Part

It's also possible for the historical results to be even better than the forward testing, because of the method in which the test was carried out. A lot of people don't really know how to properly evaluate systems. We'll get into that soon, but at this point, I just want to make it clear that the current benchmark for testing strategies is about as far from correct as Saturn is from earth. On account of this terribly erroneous method of testing, what happens is results that are seriously skewed, and overly, unrealistically optimistic. What happens is the trader then goes live with a strategy, which is bound to fail them in the end.

So I guess the question on your mind is, how do you even know what to believe and what to disregard, when you're looking at historical results?

System Vendors

One of the first things you need to realize is that most system vendors don't even trade with their own money — or any money for that matter. Look, I'm going to be brutally honest here — and you can take what I'm saying to the bank — if there's anyone desperately trying to sell you signals, or some subscription, an 'exclusive' trading room, or some black box system, then chances are they absolutely cannot be trusted. Not one bit. Sure, there are a few groups and signal providers who are actually profitable. But the best assumption to have is that they're all scammy — until proven otherwise.

Maybe I sound a bit dramatic about this, but you'll discover this is actually a better mindset to have. This way, you can save your money. Think about it, if a vendor has a really fantastic system, why sell it at all? Or why sell it for a song? They ought to be trading it themselves, if it's that good to begin with, not looking to make a quick buck by marketing it to you.

The DIY Guy

So, it's possible you've already tried the vendor thing in the past, and you've discovered through personal experience what I've already shared about them. They're just scams. So you may have decided to just do it yourself, and go it alone.

There are countless platforms, which you can use to help you make your trading analysis, test your strategies, and make them better. Now, without thinking too deeply about it, it seems like this would be the best way to handle things. You can trust yourself. You've got your own ideas of what could work. Unfortunately, while having access to all the fancy software may make it look like developing your strategy is a breeze, the sad truth it really isn't.

Software vendors would like you to believe it's oh-so-simple to create profitable strategies. This is their schtick. How else are they going to get you to buy their stuff? While you think you're getting better and better at creating your winning strategy, what's really happening is you're developing a trading system that's curve-fitted, and a little too optimized. What do I mean by that? Sure, you're going to have the most amazing, mind blowing backtest results, but when you take that strategy live and trade it in real time, then the truth of the matter will smack you hard in the face. Your system was utter crap. Has always been, will always be. For the novice do-it-yourself trader.

Commodity Trading Advisors

So you've tried the system vendors. No dice. You tried to go it alone and got an epic beatdown. What's the next best, logical option? You might begin to think about getting someone else to give you signals, or to give you a system that actually works. So you turn to a system or signals which your broker generously provides. You turn to the Commodity Trading Advisor, or CTA, for short. What are the pros? What are the cons? Let's see.

Some brokers will allow you access to their signals, for a monthly fee, from a signal provider. Usually, the signal provider also has an account with the broker, just like you do. They place live trades, which means when you look at the results, you're looking **actually** results in **real time** trading conditions. This is a big step up from the pretty picture vendors try to sell you, or the curve fitted results you get going it alone.

But here's the rub — those results still don't mean you're going to get the same level of success. Yes, I'm asking you to think of real time results as hypothetical as well. Basically, what I'm saying is unless it's your own account you're looking at, then you must absolutely view all results as hypothetical. The reason for this is there will always be some sort of variation from what you're seeing on the signal provider's account. That's just one of the cons of using a broker's services.

What else could go wrong with using signals supplied by your broker? There's a chance that **anything** really could go wrong. It could be either with the signal provider, or even your broker. For instance, if your signal provider is a discretionary trader, and they happen to go through some crises, that might throw off their trading. That's definitely going to have a negative impact on your account. On the broker's end, if they're shady, you might experience quick and sudden movements, such as a widening of the spreads, which take you out of your trade (stop hunts) or wipe your account clean, especially if you weren't using proper risk management.

You might not have to worry too much about your broker, if you did as I suggested and made sure to choose one that's regulated. A good broker will go through regular audits by accounting firms and regulators. Just be careful, because despite regulations, it's very possible for a few rotten eggs to make it into the crate. They start off looking really stellar, but then it all goes to hell when they're revealed to be extremely fraudulent. Think Bernie Madoff and his firm. His investment company was trusted and of good repute. Until it wasn't.

The <u>Experienced</u> DIY Guy

You've tried trading systems from vendors. They're crap. You know that now. You tried to do it on your own with no idea what you were really doing. Didn't work out. You tried out your CTA, but you're just not feeling too safe and sure with someone else telling you what to do. What's next?

The one option you can trust above all others is an experienced DIY developer of trading systems. What's the difference between the experienced trader and the novice? The experienced trading system developer knows and understands their backtesting software like the back of their hand. They also know all the various wrenches they can throw in the works, to see how their system handles them. They know how to fool their software. They understand the limitations posed by the software, and know how to work around said limitations. Where the trading system vendor is on the lookout for those limitations, so they can present you with a pretty looking equity curve, the experienced DIY trader is looking for ways to avoid those limitations tainting her true results.

As an experienced DIY trading system developer, you're the one in charge. You handle the entire process. You can identify the issues you may come up against, and you know how to do away with them effectively. You understand that there's such a thing as inaccurate market data, or even missing data. You know the dangers of over optimization.

I should point out that it isn't years of developing trading systems which makes you an expert. It's the ability to develop a system that proves itself in real time, over time. With enough time, you'll get even better at generating historical results, which are a truer representation of your strategy's profitability. You'll also be better at generating systems, which stand the test of time and changing market conditions.

Why Test?

A valid question. Since, in general, historical results are not necessarily a true picture of future trading outcomes, it only makes sense that there's no point testing this anyway, right? Well, you're right. Sort of.

While this disclaimer is attached to every single trading system, that doesn't mean historical data is completely useless. For instance, say you'd like to construct a model of the number of hours in each day. So each day, you run calculations of just how many hours there are. You do this for a whole month. Without fail, each day is 24 hours long. Net, you decide to create a model, which will predict the number of hours each day will have, based on one month's worth of historical data you have amassed.

Will the next day still have 24 hours? How can you tell for sure? It's possible some cosmic event could occur, changing the length of days as we know it. It's also highly unlikely. But you know what else was highly unlikely? That insane Brexit crash. The recent silver flash crash. 2010's flash crash. 2008's financial crisis. The point is, it's possible for these events, which do not conform to expectations to happen.

So what happens to your model when faced with such issues? Does this then render your model invalid? Of course not! What happens now is you know you need to factor in the new changes in market behavior. While your model may be rendered obsolete by some cataclysmic change in the markets at any moment, it's still worth it to have a model based off of historical data, than to simply play a guessing game with the market. If you guess, you might find yourself confused when the day ends with 24 hours, versus your sure bet of 72.

What are some of the ways we can obtain results from the evaluation of our trading system? There are four ways to do this: backtesting, walk forward testing, out-of-sample testing, and real time testing.

Historical Backtesting

This is the method of testing everyone and their grandma is most familiar with. It's super easy to carry out, and is even easier to abuse.

When backtesting, what you need to do is specify the time period you'd like to go over. There's an option for you to enter the start date, and end date. The end date, more often than not, is whenever the last, most recent tick available on your chart is. Backtesting also has a few other parameters, which you can optimize. When all that is set up, your strategy tester will do its thing, and you'll receive results for the set period of time, with your particular parameters. Then you may go on to test your strategy in a live market.

As easy as that sounds, there are a lot of issues to contend with when carrying out backtesting this way. Your results may look good, but might actually be overly optimized — meaning you've got way too many rules and parameters, so of course, the historical result is going to look great! You've essentially set up parameters that are designed to get the most beautiful looking equity curve — off of previous data. Going forward with real time price action, there's no way that the market will exactly mirror what you've tested back in the past.

With backtesting, you want to keep in mind that the more rules and parameters you set up, the more you optimize your system, the less likely it will do well in future market conditions. The truth remains that backtesting is the domain of the most inexperienced traders, the ones who are extremely naive and gullible. I'm not trying to make you feel like an idiot. I'm simply stating the truth. If this is the way you've always tested your systems, chances are you haven't been getting results in live trading as good as the results you got from your backtest. I've been there too. I know what I'm talking about.

Out-of-Sample Testing

How do you deal with the problems of backtesting? One way to handle this is by adding an out-of-sample period, which ideally should be anywhere from 10% to 20% of the data you'll be reviewing, once you're done with optimizing.

Usually, the most recent data is what is used for out-of-data sampling — although there are some traders who use this testing with pre-optimized data. So where you have the results for your backtest looking like they'll give you the fattest, sexiest account balance going forward, by the time you test out the strategy on the out-of-sample data, what you will find is closer to the actual types of results you'd get, were you to go live with that strategy. This is a way better approach than just optimizing all the data you have, as it paints a truer picture of what to expect. When you've got a situation where the results you've optimized look really great, alongside the out-of-sample data, then you most likely have a system, which will do, good in live trading conditions as well.

Walk Forward Testing

This is a lot more than your average backtest. It takes a lot more effort in order to conduct a walk forward test of your system, but I assure you, it is very worth it in the end. You can do walk forward testing manually, along with your trusty trading software optimization. Before you attempt using software, do try to do this manually for a while, so you can understand what goes on during the process.

So what exactly is walk forward testing about? In this method, what you need to know is the optimized results as well as the performance results have two kinds of data sets as their foundations. What you'll be working with is a number of out-of-sample periods, all lumped together.

When you make use of walk forward testing, you tend to get results, which are as true as they can be to what you'll get trying your strategy out in real time trading. Often, there is rarely any difference between the results from the out-of-sample periods, and those from live market trades.

Be warned though, this really is no walk in the park. You need access to an impressive size of past data to make this happen. However, I cannot recommend this method of testing enough. When you don't have enough data to go by, though, what can you do?

Real Time Testing

A few of the most successful traders don't even bother with backtesting — for all those reasons we've already gone over. So what they do instead is test out their strategies in live market conditions. I mean real time trading, and even then, they test with real money — since the feeds and spreads on a demo accounts tend to be somewhat different from the live ones.

There's a lot to be said for testing in real time. For instance, there's no way you're creating rules to fit data that's already in the past. You can't over optimize here. The drawback to using this method of testing is that you can only move as fast as the market and time do. You can't quite gather the stats for your strategy over a period of years... Without testing for a period of years. As such, it's a bit of a stretch to find traders with this much patience to test out their strategy.

There is another downside to this, which is if you change the strategy a bit, tweak one parameter or the other, then you're basically going to have to start from scratch. All the data you gathered before making those tweaks are now rendered invalid. This means more months, or even years of testing, before you know whether or not you really do have a solid strategy to run with. While it takes a lot of time and effort, in the end, testing done in real time is absolutely the best way to verify you've got a working trading system.

Chapter 6: Initial Analysis

Now you know all you need to know about how to test your strategy, let's dive into the most important bits of the reports generated at the end of your testing phase. Most strategy performance reports can be ridiculously long, with all sorts of information packed in. Quite frankly, this can be a bit much.

You've got all sorts of parameters, graphs, trade lists... all well into the hundreds. The funny thing is this information overload is unnecessary and inefficient, and some parameters are quite unnecessary — at least, not for when I'm trading my own systems.

When trading, the need for simplicity cannot be overstressed. The same applies to trading reports. You only need a few of the parameters measured, not the whole enchilada.

First things first, you want to make sure your report is based off of a walk forward test, or a real time test to begin with. Any other thing is not likely to give you a true representation. Next, you need to make sure your test covered several years of data, and that there are at least 30 trades (100, even!) for each parameter of your trading system. Another thing is the size of the positions trades. You can't expect to compare reports on strategies that use several contracts in sizing positions, to those, which only use a single contract. It would be like comparing apples to onions. As a good rule of thumb, you want to consider the size of the positions, if and only if the strategy has proven to be worth its sale when you use a single contract for all trades.

Last but not least, you need to factor in slippage and commissions in your report. This is not optional. You absolutely must! I stress this because time and time again, I see a lot of analysis reports in which the system's creator didn't bother to factor in the spreads, slippage, and commission. Usually, they are of the opinion that these things can always be factored in later without a hitch.

Slippage and Commissions Matter

Let me be very clear about this, not only is not considering these trading costs downright unethical, it's a huge red flag that the creator of the strategy truly doesn't even understand how to make a proper one! To give an example, let us say you were optimizing your strategy based off of net profit, or something of the sort. What you're going to get from the optimizer is a set of rules, which might encourage you, overtrade.

Let's take a look at an analysis, which does not factor in slippage or commissions. Say you've got two different parameters — **parameter 1**, and **parameter 2**.

In parameter 1, your gross profit per trade equals $30. So when you take 1,000 profitable trades, your gross profit is $30,000.

In parameter 2, your gross profit per trade equals $60. Take 400 trades, and your gross profit is $24,000.

Naturally, your optimizer will select parameter 1 as the better of the two. But what happens when you've got at least $30 in commissions and slippage?

According to parameter 1, your net profit per trade is actually $0. Take a thousand trades, a million even, and your net profit remains $0.

With parameter 2, your net profit per trade is $30. When you take 400 trades, you actually make a net profit is $12,000.

In this case, parameter 2 is clearly king! So you tell me — which way is actually better? Which way would supply the most profits? Which way would leave the trader at breakeven at best, with a lot of wasted time and effort, or at worst, with a steadily depleting account? As you can see, slippage and commissions do matter. The second case is obviously much closer to real time trading, than the first case. So whenever you're optimizing, please do account for slippage and commissions.

Total Net Profit

The next most important thing to look out for is the total net profit. It seems pretty obvious, doesn't it? What's the point of bothering with the trading system's analysis report, if there's no recorded profits? Whether it was a case of there being barely enough of net profit, or it was a matter of having to endure ridiculous amounts of drawdown before seeing any substantial profits doesn't matter. There has to be profit, or there is no point.

When doing a walk forward test, the very least a system should generate should be about $5,000 per year, for each contract. If it does even more than that, then that's even better.

Profit Factor

This is the next thing to go over. It goes without saying that the higher the profit factor of your walk forward test, the better. You want a profit factor, which is at the very least 1.0. It's not enough to discard a system just because you think a factor of 1.0 is too small. However, there's a higher chance that profit factors lower than 1.0 will not sale through the system development process quite as easy as the higher ones.

Number of Trades

It's important to also consider the number of trades. You need to make sure that there were enough trades executed according to your algos parameters, for you to come to sound decisions regarding your trading system. If you only took about a dozen trades, you can't expect the results to be so solid. However, if you took at least thirty to a hundred trades per each parameter, you'd have a more accurate picture. If you have 5 rules or parameters, for example, you should have at least 150 to 500 trades in your final report. If you've got even more trades, than that's even better!

Average Trade Net Profits

This is just as important as the slippage and commissions. If you want an easy peasy way to figure out just how profitable your strategy is against another, then this is the figure you need to look out for. For each trading contract, $50 or even more would be ideal, as the average trade net profit. Anything less, and you're dangerously close to breakeven territory — even if your system is viable, somewhat. When this is the case, there is less margin for errors and seemingly minute changes in results.

Average Losing Trades

Your average losing trade is a number to consider, because comparing that with the average trade net profit, you'll be able to accurately calculate the expectancy of your strategy. The usual way most traders calculate expectancy is to multiply the average amount of winners (in dollars) by the win percentage, and then add that to the result of the dollar amount of average losers multiplied by the loss percentage, which would then equal the average trade. Here, the average losers would be a negative number.

What you get following that formula is still the average trade net profit. So attempting to calculate expectancy based on that formula will not give you any further information than what you already know. A more useful way to calculate expectancy would be to first multiply the average $ winners by the win percentage, then multiply the average $ losers by the loss percentage, and then add those figures. Next, you'd divide the results by the negative average $

losers. This would prove much better than the former, since it's actually adjusted for risk. It lets you know what you expect to gain for each dollar you risk in your trades. If your expectancy is 0.4, then that means you gain 40 cents for each $1 you risk. Dr. Van Tharp, an educator and psychologist, is an avid supporter of this expectancy calculation method.

With this method, you want your strategy to have values, which are above 0.1. If you trade any strategy with an expectancy below 0.1, it would be pointless. You might as well park your money in the bank, where at least you'd get some interest annually, because the risk simply would not be worth the reward.

Total Slippage and Total Commission

Bearing in mind all we've talked about beforehand about slippage and commission, if the number for this is $0, then that report is utterly useless, and no other elements of the report are worth taking a look at. I'll give you one guess why I say this. It's simple. **There's really no such thing as zero trading costs.** If you happen to see a performance analysis, which shows no trading costs, then toss it. It's crap.

At the very minimum, when it comes to commissions, you can expect $5 for each round turn trade per contract. That's usually the average amount your broker will charge. Commissions can be a lot less however, if you trade high volumes, or you are a member of an exchange. However, for most retail traders, it's at least $5.

Even more important than total commission is the total slippage. If you have ever had the opportunity to observe newbie developers who haven't even placed a single trade, they tend to grossly underestimate just how much slippage happens in live trading conditions. What really is slippage? It's the difference between the price your backtesting software fills your orders in at, and the price your fills would be in a real trading scenario.

For instance, it's assumed by many strategy development engines that your long orders are filled at the bid, while your short orders are filled at the ask. However, in real market conditions, chances are you'll actually be triggered into longs at the ask, and triggered into shorts at the bid. This difference is what we refer to as slippage.

When you're dealing with stocks, which are traded heavily, you'll find that your slippage is usually about 1 or 2 ticks per round turn for market orders, and 1 or 2 ticks per round turn for stop orders as well. As for limit orders, there's usually no slippage.

So the trick here would be to develop a strategy, which uses a nice blend of stop, limit, and market orders. When applying slippage value to each trade in this scenario, it would be best to play conservatively. So what you want to do is account for 1.5 to 2 ticks of slippage for strategies, which employ this blend of orders. Is it a glass-half-empty way of looking at things? Perhaps. But it's much better to be safe, than to be severely disappointed with the live trading results.

Maximum Drawdown

Let's assume for a moment that you're testing a strategy with your algos, which yields a net profit of $35,000 and a maximum drawdown of $30,000. Would you trade that? Of course you wouldn't. Everything is wrong with this strategy. While you're at it, you might as well resort to flipping a coin before you take your trades. You might have even better chances at winning then.

When you see the figures representing maximum drawdown in a report, you want to keep in mind that there's a possibility of the drawdown being even worse than was indicated! It goes without saying that you need to put that strategy to sleep. Permanently.

There are other figures, which are just as important in your strategy's performance report. There are people who deem the winning percentage to be important. There are some who find the Sharpe ratio to be of invaluable help to them. I'm not saying that other metrics besides the ones I've mentioned here are not important. They all are, to a certain point. It's your job as a developer to figure out what figures you're good with. In the end, what really matters is whatever metrics you do choose to focus on, they all help you develop a truly winning strategy, which works great in real time trading.

Closed Trade Equity Graph

Having reviewed all the relevant figures, one thing to take a look at next is the closed trade equity graph. For the trader who favors visuals, a close look at an equity curve will let you know everything worth knowing. What should you look for in an equity chart, you wonder?

The Slope

First things first, consider the slope. If your chart is not making steady progress from the bottom left to the top right, then this might not be a strategy you want to use. Bear in mind that you might find the true story a closed trade equity graph tells could be skewed by the scaling used on the graph. So another thing to do besides look, is divide the final equity by the number of years displayed in the curve. This is the best way for you to gauge the actually average profit per annum, and know whether or not this is a strategy worth investing your time in.

The Flats

The next thing to consider after slopes are the flat periods in the graph. Flats are better than dips caused by drawdown, obviously, but if you have too many flats occasionally broken up with sharp rises, then you may want to hold off a bit on announcing your discovery of the Holy Grail. It's quite likely that what's happening in this scenario is your system is only getting a handful of good, profitable trades — and that this only happens because you have overly optimized your system, or there has been some curve fitting.

Not all flat periods should give cause for concern though. Some of them may be caused by outside, unavoidable circumstances, such as the United States government's introduction of quantitative easing programs from 2009 to 2013. Here, you could make the assumption that over a matter of time, the performance of your strategy will indeed be better whenever the government wraps up the intervention. When the government might make that decision of course is entirely unpredictable.

The Drawdown

Yet another important thing to look at, you need to know how bad the drawdowns are in your strategy, and you also need to find out how long periods of drawdown last. It's also important to note how long it takes your system to bounce back from the drawdowns. Once you know all this, you have a somewhat solid grasp of what you can expect if you take your strategy live. Do keep in mind that the drawdown in the future, in live market conditions, could be even worse than what your reports have revealed. The way to survive drawdown is to make use of reasonable risk and money management.

If you're looking at the equity curve, and you don't even see a hunt of drawdown that is not the Holy Grail. I repeat, that is not the Holy Grail! There is something deeply flawed with the system, and you need to look into it. The only system, which yields you steady profits with no drawdown, would be the system of stashing your money in a savings account. There is no risk without reward. There is no such thing as an equity curve that only goes up, ever.

Fuzzy Stuff

One more thing to look at, when observing your equity curve, is a little thing I like to refer to as its 'fuzziness.' You might not see this on a closed equity graph, but you can see it on a daily equity graph. A really fuzzy curve indicates that the day to day results are constantly all over the place, moving up and down in the shorter term, despite the longer term trend being up.

If you notice your curve is fuzzy, then there's a huge chance your system is hard to trade, it's hard to properly size positions, and it's a real tough one to deal with, emotionally speaking. To put things in perspective, which of these systems would you prefer?

System 1:
Day 1 = +$300. Day 2 = -$300. Day 3 = + $125. Day 4 = -$115.
System 2:
Day 1 = +$35. Day 2 = +$35. Day 3 = +$35. Day 4 = +$35.

I do hope you chose system 2. If you chose system 1, listen: you shouldn't be trading. Go bungee jumping if you're looking for thrills, you daredevil.

Now, I'm not suggesting that simply looking at an equity curve is enough to evaluate a trading system's profitability over the long haul — but it is useful in your initial analysis of your trading system. How? If the equity curve of a system looks iffy, then you don't need to even bother with the rest of the report. This saves you time and dollars.

Chapter 7: In-Depth Analysis

As you further develop your trading strategy, the need for analysis continues to rise. The parameters by which you measure the worth of your strategy also become even stricter. One of the best ways to ensure you have a trustworthy strategy, is by making use of in-depth analysis — specifically, Monte Carlo analysis.

The Process of Monte Carlo Analysis

Give some thought to the trades you've taken in accordance with your strategy. Think of each standalone trade, not the aggregate of your trades. The sequence of the trades is what actually creates your equity curve. The question now is, if you were to vary the order in which your trades were taken, how would the equity curve be different? Would your drawdown become even worse, or better? What would be the end equity — the same as before, or much different? Using Monte Carlo analysis, you'll have all the answers to these questions.

A Simple Exercise

Get some paper, and then tear them up into little bits. On each piece, go on and write down a trade result. Do this until you have all trade results recorded. Next, put all the pieces of paper in a bowl or something, and then pull one of them out at random. Let us assume what you pulled out is your very first trade. Go on and record it, by adding it to your beginning equity. Then put the paper back in the bowl. What you're doing right now is called 'random sampling with replacement.'

Next, pick up another piece of paper, and then record the value. Add it to your new equity. Continue with this, as many times as you can. When you're through, you should have a whole slew of equity curves — each of which show you the various ways your strategy could have worked out (or not).

With these new equity curves, you'll be able to get all the stats on your trading system. You'll be able to perform a better evaluation of your strategy, figure out the best position sizes to use for each trade relative to your equity, and have an even more realistic picture of the possibilities you could come face to face when you do decide to take your strategy and apply it to actually trading conditions, live. Do keep in mind that doing this is based on the assumption that the trades you made in the past will be more or less the same as the trades you'll make in the future. Why do I say this? To remind you that if your historical results were flawed to begin with, then you can expect your future results to be even more so.

The Drawbacks

There are a few cons to consider with this sort of analysis — the obvious one being the erroneous assumption that you'll be making the exact same trades going forward. When you do put a trade on, anything can happen, despite your best intentions and your meticulous observation of all your rules.

That said, if you've got an accurate distribution of trades — both mean and standard deviation — then making use of the Monte Carlo analysis can indeed prove to be very fruitful.

Yet another drawback to consider is that the analysis is based on the assumption that each trade has no connection to the previous trade. Usually, for a lot of strategies, this is not necessarily a problem. If, however, your strategy relies on trades being dependent on one another, then the good old fashioned Monte Carlo analysis is quite simply not the best route to go.

For example, you could have a strategy where the next trading signal depends on the result of the previous trade. If this is the case, then you definitely do not need to use Monte Carlo analysis as is. What you would need to get the stats you're looking for would be a kind of analytical method known as 'moving start analysis.' How would this play out?

First, you create a simulation of the beginning of your trading session with each trade. Next, you get all the stats regarding your drawdown and return. Say you had 12 trades, from $i, i + 1, \ldots i + 11$ in your chosen sample, then you'd need to have an equity curve which begins with i.

From the curve, it's easy to deduce the drawdown d_i. The next step is to begin the equity curve again with trade $i + 1$, which would then give you the drawdown $d_i + 1$. When you're through with all the trades like this, then you can go over the sets of drawdowns. Yes, this is a lot more painstaking than the Monte Carlo method, but this is the only way to go about things when your strategy involves the serial correlation of trades.

If you've found that you can cope with the drawback of the Monte Carlo system of analysis, the good news is it will help you figure out what your kind of returns you can expect from your system per annum, whether you have the best risk to reward ratio, what the chances are that you'll have a max drawdown of a certain percentage, and what the risk of ruin is for the size of the account you're trading.

Monte Carlo Simulator Inputs

In order to properly execute a Monte Carlo simulation, you're going to need a few inputs.

Base Initial Equity: This is the initial equity in your account before you commence trading, in dollars.

Cease Trading if or when Equity drops below $: This is straightforward. It's the amount below which your algorithm will stop executing trades. If your equity dips below the set amount of dollars, all trading will cease, as your account is basically 'ruined,' or as most traders like to say, 'blown.' The value you set here has to be much higher than the initial margin for a single contract of whatever stock you're trading. To trade instruments, which require a higher margin, then it would be wise to increase this value. To be safe though, never trade with only just enough equity to cover the margin required for your chosen instrument.

Number of Trades Over 1 Year: This is basically the amount of trades your algo will execute over a period of a year. You can set up your simulator to trade for just a year, so each equity curve you do generate will consist of the number of trades you have programmed in this parameter. It will hit this number, provided you haven't ruined your account before the year is over.

Results of Individual Trades: The data here will consist of everything relevant to each trade that has been executed, based on the same points of reference, daily, for each contract, etc. You won't be able to blend single contract trades and multi-contract trades here.

Monte Carlo Simulation Limitations

First off, the assumption is that each trade is one contract only. There's no consideration for the size of positions in the simulator. Another thing is the simulator really only focuses on a year of trading, and no more. If you do know your way around macro programming language, then you can easily change the Excel macro code to change these base assumptions of the simulation.
Now, we're going to go over a 'run', which is basically the process of creating one equity curve. In any given simulation, there will be a certain number of runs. For the Monte Carlo simulation, the number of runs would be 2,500, which helps analyze the relevant stats concerning the risk of ruin, among other things.

Monte Carlo Simulation Output

When the simulation has been successfully completed, it will spit out a bunch of output values, as well as equity curves. Here are some of those values, and their interpretations. These values are important in fashioning a highly tradable system.

Initial Equity: This is the equity in your account before running the Monte Carlo analysis. Your risk of ruin, rates of return, and max drawdown are all connected to this amount.

Risk of Ruin: This is the likelihood that your account will be blown within a year's time — that is, the chances that it will be triggered by the instruction to cease trading when your equity goes below a certain dollar amount. If your risk of ruin is 155, that means, within a year, there's a 15% percent likelihood of your account being ruined.

This is one stat that is extremely important, especially for traders with relatively small account sizes. The risk of ruin, while barely having any effect on a larger account, would definitely hit a smaller account harder — even if you have an amazing system that rakes in huge wins! The fact of the matter is you need to have enough funds to trade. No matter how stellar your system is, it can be completely and utterly disastrous for you to jump into the markets severely underfunded.

Generally speaking, if the risk of ruin is above 10%, it means you need more capital than you're trading with to make this work, and still get impressive rates of return.

Median Drawdown: This is the median of the max drawdown. Understand that the max drawdown is simply the maximum percentage by which your account size drops from an equity peak. This is usually calculated based on the last equity peak. For each run of the simulation, you will experience a maximum percentage drawdown. When you've got a lot of runs, you'll also have the max drawdowns distributed, and this will vary from 100 percent (completely wrecked account) to 0% (a dream which does not exist).

There will be a median value, where the drawdown values go over the median by 50%, and go below it by 50% as well. So, the median maximum drawdown is basically the middle ground of the aggregate of maximum drawdowns over a large series of runs.

If you're a fairly new trader, then you need to beware of your tendency to overestimate your ability to handle drawdowns. Cut your expectations in half. This way, you're less likely to give up on what's actually a working system, or give in to the urge to change this and tweak that.

Median $ Profit: This is the equity you end up with, subtracted from the equity you began with, after a year of trades. In this case, since we're talking about 2,500 runs of the simulation, we can then easily calculate the median level. This is known as the median $ profit.

Median Return: This is calculated just as the median $ profit, but the ending equity will be divided by the starting equity, in order to arrive at the percentage of median returns. It's best to aim for returns above 50%.

Return to Drawdown Ratio: This is easily one of the most significant numbers generated by the Monte Carlo analysis. It's also known as the Calmar ratio, when calculated over a period of three years. This number is generated by dividing the median annual percentage by the median maximum percentage drawdown.

Prob > 0: Written as a percentage, this is the probability of your system making money in the first year of trading. Obviously, the higher the percentage, the better your system is.

Chapter 8: Creating Your System

There are a whole lot of trading system software available today — NinjaTrader, MultiCharts, TradeStation, cTrader, among so many others. This is what I like to call a 'blurse' — a blessing and a curse.

On the plus side, these amazing programs have made it easier than ever to turn an idea into a strategy. Where it used to take weeks and even months to create a great strategy using Excel or some really tough programming language such as C, C++, Visual Basic, and even Fortran, it now can all happen with just a few clicks. So that's awesome.

One the flip side, though, there's the fact that there are millions of traders who are testing out all sorts of trading ideas, and if you do discover any edge, so will they. This makes that so called edge useless. Another thing is that it makes the process way too easy. All you need to do is simply insert any prepackaged strategy that came with the program, and then you can begin with your over optimization and curve fitting — which, as we've already established, are terrible for developing a winning strategy. Sure, you're going to have a backtest that's a beauty to behold. But when it goes live, it's going to hell.

Yet another downside to the oversimplification of the strategy development process by these programs, is that professional traders who know what they're doing won't even bother with them. If the professional trader won't use these programs, then that should surely make you wonder if they're really worth it,

The pros use tools, which are a lot more complicated than these programs. I'm talking about stuff like Matlab, Python, R, and others. Either that, or they're working on creating their own platforms from open source codes freely available on the net. This doesn't necessarily mean this is the only way to go. It's just that you need to be aware that these programs, despite their appeal, do have their cons.

It's necessary for you to put in the time if you want to succeed, or else the markets will completely humble you. Like a school bully who takes all your lunch money. It's imperative that you get smart about the way you develop your systems, and create a step by step approach. You can't afford to skip any steps.

In the process of creating your strategy, if you find yourself encountering failures, you can simply make adjustments as you go along, or move on to a different strategy with more promise. The second option is the better option, because usually, when a strategy fails the first go around, there are chances that whatever changes made would encourage curve fitting, with a great looking backtest. Recall though, that the goal is not to have a great set of results from your backtest, but to create a backtest that will represent a true image of what future results might look like when following your strategy.

Tips for Creating Your Strategy

When you come across a strategy, which you find interesting, note it down. You want to make a habit of writing down the ideas, which occur to you. Be sure to look anywhere and everywhere for strategy ideas. You can look at books on trading, magazines, and popular internet blogs and forums. Don't just take the ideas presented and trade them as is. Instead, see how you can make it your own.

Understand that there is no such thing as a stupid idea. An idea is only stupid if it remains untested. So be sure to test, test, and test again, and learn to easily discard what does not work.

If you find you have made a huge error in the process of coding your algo, still go ahead and test it out anyway. Sometimes, these "errors" are actually your subconscious mind at work, creating something that will definitely work for you. Yes, it may sound a bit far out, but there are treasures to be found in mistakes.

When you find your trades simply are not playing out like they should, try being counterintuitive. Do you see a reason to buy? Then go short instead. Does that look like a juicy short? Go ahead and buy. You might be surprised what you'll find out in the process of being counterintuitive or counter logical.

Commit to testing out a strategy or at most five each week. It could take you months, or a year, or more than a year. But you'll definitely discover gold, sooner or later.

Running out of ideas? Then just take a look at the charts. Just stare at them. If you like slap on an indicator. Maybe two. Don't try to think. Leave the charts for a bit, and then come back to them days later, or weeks later. When you come back, you can begin to ask yourself what it is you see that connects the indicator to the chart, or what you've noticed on the chart. Note down what you notice, and then program it and test it out.

Look for other traders who are about the same level as you are, in terms of skills. You can all swap strategies and bounce ideas off of each other. You could try building strategies around the other traders' ideas. This is a great way to keep you sharp, and you might come up with some of the most brilliant strategies yet!

Don't be afraid to change the criteria you trade with. You might be being a little too closed minded. Try it all. You can take a look a t other strategies which are a bridge between what your criteria are, and what they aren't. This isn't to say you must trade the strategies as they prove themselves to you. What you'll be achieving here is getting more confident in your ability to develop great systems. Once you've done this, you may then begin to get stricter about your criteria, and then you'll eventually make your strategy more rock solid than it was in the beginning. In no time, you'll have a working strategy, which lines up with all the requirements you originally had.

Optimizing Your Strategy

Yes, you will do this. But the point is to know the limits. The truth is you can't really develop a strategy without doing some measure of optimizing. Say you begin with testing out a bajillion strategies. Chances are more than a handful of them are going to scale through and pass your every test, proving themselves to be potential winners.

When this happens, you'll have an actually edge. You can trust that you'll be profitable with it, unless and until the edge is gone. Another possible outcome is you discover you may have overdone it with the optimizing, but you don't have anything that shows it will actually work in real time. Or, you may have tested all strategies possible, and found one or two which pass your tests, but in the end they don't really give you an edge in live trading conditions. My guess is you'd rather have the first scenario to be the case.

If you want to avoid finding strategies, which seem to have an edge (only to turn out to be utterly useless in the end) you need to have a logical reason behind your chosen strategy. Give some thought to your entries and exits, and how you might be able to gain an edge from them. See how best you can take advantage of the market.

Do your best to keep it stupid simple. Usually, when you have rules, rules, and more rules, what happens is that your strategy will not work out well in the long run. Another thing you want to avoid is simply slapping on all sorts of indicators until you find something that clicks for you. When you do all sorts of tests like this, chances are you will find something, but there is most likely going to be a snag somewhere. While there are some programs, which do employ the slap-on-random-indicator technique, and they actually can be used to give you something useful, it's best to use your own head. Your computer is not going to do all the thinking on your behalf. Remember: **garbage in, garbage out.**

SMART Development

In order to develop efficient systems, you have to set goals. **SMART** goals. Chances are you already know where I'm headed with this. Your goals have got to be **S**pecific, **M**easurable, **A**ttainable, **R**elevant, **T**ime bound.

Specific

You are bound to fail if your goals are vague. It isn't enough to desire "a trading system that makes a ton of money," or "a risk free trading system." Those goals are not only vague, but are simply unrealistic. Why? There's really no way to determine when you've reached these goals. What's "a ton of money?" How do you truly define "risk free?"

Measurable

If a goal you set is not measurable, then you won't achieve much. You'd simply be a hamster on a wheel, moving, but going nowhere. By the time you're through developing and testing your system, you should be able to match your goals to the performance reports you get from testing it. "I want to create a system that beats anything out there" is admirable, but not measurable. You don't know every trading system out there. You can't measure this goal.

Attainable

"I'm going to develop a system where I risk only 1 tick and bag 1,000 ticks per trade, for every trading day." This is clearly a pipe dream. It's just not going to happen. I'm not trying to be a negative Nancy, but that's just the way the cookie crumbles. You need to shoot for a goal that's plausible and attainable. If you don't, you're setting yourself up for frustration, disappointment, and defeat.

Relevant

There is absolutely no gain in creating a system, if you don't see the relevance to begin with. If you hate everything you need to do to develop a working system, you need to sit down and ask yourself if you really should be doing this. If you're going to be successful, then you need to make a decision, and commit to it. Otherwise, there's just no point. In trading, there are those who 'sorta' want it, and those who **really want it.** Which camp do you belong to? Be honest with yourself. There's nothing wrong with quitting something your heart really isn't into anyway.

Time Bound

Let's face it, the whole process of developing a successful trading system is time consuming. The best way to avoid being totally buried under the whole process is to set aside some time to create your strategy, and also give yourself a deadline for each idea you spend time on. This way, you can keep the whole thing moving, rather than beat a dead horse over and over till it resurrects itself only to grab the whip and beat you in return. It's important to put a time limit, because what you'll realize over time is it's pretty difficult to stay motivated when you've tested hundreds of ideas, and they all fail you.

What SMART Goals Look Like

You could say, "I am going to develop a trading system which satisfies my objectives." Already, with all we've discussed so far, you can see that this is not a specific goal. What about it being attainable? It would seem to be. Is it relevant? Yes, it is. Is it time bound? No, it isn't. This goal clearly needs some optimizing.

What if you said, "I am going to develop a trading system in 5 months, which satisfies my objectives?" Now it's still not more specific than just "create a trading system." Everyone creates trading systems all the time. What's different about yours? Also, you cannot measure this goal. However, it is possible to attain. 5 months of hard work should get you a system. It's relevant. Also, it's definitely time bound. Now, how could we tighten up this goal?

"I am going to create a trading system within five months; the system will trade the GOOGL stock, give an average return of 60% per annum, have a drawdown of 24% maximum, a win percentage of 55% and up, and go through every step in a proper development process." Now, as DJ Khaled would say, "You smart!"

Now with this goal in place, once you begin, you might make a few interesting discoveries. One of them might be that the goals which you originally thought would be easy to attain are not quite so. What do you do? **Get SMARTER.** So you're going to **E**valuate the goals you have set, and then you will **R**evaluate them. Again. This is called adaptability. If you find yourself struggling to attain the goal you set, just cut that goal in half and try for that instead. This will exponentially improve the odds of your finding a good system.

Chapter 9: Your Trade System Idea

Now you've got your goals properly figured out, the smarter way, so you can get to work developing your system. Before you move on, there are a few things you'll need to cover first, so you have an idea what your trading system will be like. You need to know what your entry and exit signals are. You need to pick the stocks you'll be trading. Also, it's important to determine the time frame or bar size you'll focus on, and take into consideration the programming process and the data available to you.

Entering The Market

Figuring out how to get into the market is not hard at all. It's the easiest bit in creating a trading system. It's also what most newbie traders focus on the most. They think once you've got that figured out, the rest of it is pretty much sorted. But it doesn't quite work that way. Their focus is on making sure they have as little drawdown as possible — everything else doesn't matter, as far as they're concerned. I know. I've been there.

Why does the entry point seem to be what fascinates these traders the most about a system? The entry is just about the only thing you can control in a trade. At the point of entry, you're the one calling the shots. You aren't going to click a single button unless and until the market has met your entry requirements. That's just about the only predictable bit about trading the markets. Compare that to the flood of emotions you feel once you're in the trade, hoping it goes your way so you can breathe easy again.

F0r some reason, everyone thinks that entries are more important than any other thing in your trading system. Remember Dr. Van Tharp, though? There was a study he did where he jumped into the market with random entries, and was able to create a bunch of trading systems, which did well by simply being careful about his exits. That's not to say you can't make money with random exits, though.

The entry only matters depending on what sort of trader you are. For instance, entries would matter a hell of a lot more to the scalper who is only in trades for seconds or minutes at a time, than they would matter to the swing trader who holds trades for weeks and months. For the scalper, entering at the wrong price would turn an amazing system into epic pile of trash. For the swing trader, entering at random probably wouldn't affect how profitable she gets over the long term. This fact is important to remember when you're developing your system. Recall you're developing an algo, and that there is no room for discretionary trading here. So program your entries accordingly.

Having figured out your entry rules, you want to then translate them into a computer language. Chances are you're not so great at programming. That's fine. You can always hire a programmer to help you out with this — after you've put your idea into a 'pseudo code.' For example: "If daily candle closes above previous daily candle, buy at market on open of the next candle."

Tips for Good Entries

Keep it simple. If you're unable to explain it in good old fashioned English, then chances are it will be difficult to code your entry rules. Another good rule of thumb is to keep the number of parameters to a minimum. There's always the temptation to go overboard with your parameters, but the more you add, the more you're likely to over optimize your strategy. So keep things as simple as possible. 1 to 2 input parameters are enough.

Do yourself a favor, and think differently. Yes, it's tempting to try to make moving average crossover strategies. Eve beginning trader figures they're the easiest, and they ought to be profitable strategies. The question to ask yourself, if you want to go down that road, is how can you make yours different? What uniqueness can you bring to the moving average table?

Finally, when you first start off, make use of just one simple rule. Sure, you may want to add in other conditions as well, but start with just the one. As you test, you'll see whether or not you need to add others in, and you'll be able to gauge if they actually improve your system, or if they're just unnecessary complications you could do without.

Exiting the Market

This is the stuff most people will not bother with. Not that this is not understandable. You really have no control over what happens to a trade after you've put it on. You can't tell how long the trend will go before it reverses on you, or if your target will be hit before then. You're literally at the mercy of the market here.

Another reason traders would rather not even think about exits, is because of the psychological pain of thinking about how to deal with either losing money, or leaving money on the table. You want to make all the money, and you want it all in one trade. Well, this is newbie thinking. Sooner or later, you'll learn to take what the market offers.

It is well worth keeping in mind that exits can and do have a huge impact on how profitable your strategy is in the long run. You need to spend some time figuring out how to leave the market with your dignity and sanity intact. There are all sorts of ways to do this.

The stop and reverse exit method would basically be exiting as soon as you get a signal to enter a trade in the opposite direction. This is useful for those who love to be in the market all the time.

Technical exits are exits made as a result of decisions you arrive at from technical analysis. It could be a significant candlestick pattern at a psychological or round number, support and resistance lines and zones, moving averages, Fibonacci lines, or whatever. When using these, they have to match up with your entry rules as well. If they don't, it's possible for you to get taken out of your trade just moments after you entered.

Breakeven stops involves setting your stop loss to breakeven as soon as the trade has moved a considerable amount in your favor. This can be beneficial, psychologically speaking, as you are now 'risk free.' Of course, when placing your stops at breakeven, you need to be careful to account for the commission, spread, and swaps, if any. However, while this works great for the discretionary trader's peace of mind, I've noticed more often than not, placing stops at breakeven can severely limit your profitability. You yourself may have experienced a scenario where the trade begins to move in your favor, and then it comes back to your entry, before resuming in the direction you wanted it to go. If you had your stop at break even when it came back, then chances are you got taken out of the trade. You might not even be able to reenter, because while the price was at the same level you got in at, the other entry conditions you set up may not line up.

Stop loss exits. Some traders love them, some traders hate them. The thing to keep in mind with this though, is that if the placement of your stop loss is a problem — either being too close so you're always stopped out before the market moves your way, or too far, so you give back whatever profits you've got and a generous chunk of your initial equity — then chances are the **real** problem is actually your entry. Never trade without a stop loss. Imagine doing that during some major event like Brexit, or an election, or a terrorist attack. That could be catastrophic for you, if you happen to be in the wrong trade at the time. Stop losses will make sure you live to trade another day.

Profit targets are yet another way to exit a trade. Sure, you'll always hear it said that you should let your profits run. But this is not always the best idea. Do you have any idea where the market is going to turn around and go against you? I have a friend who always says of trading, "A bird in the hand is worth two in the bush." Sometimes, you would be better off setting a profit target, either based off of technical analysis, or based on a certain dollar amount, and then get ready to trade the next signals. Ultimately, the best strategies are those, which allow you to get the most profit targets, more often than not.

Trailing stops. If you believe in letting your profits run, then this is the best choice. As the market continues to move in your factor, you lock in a set amount of profit along the way. This is basically you moving your stop loss either over time, or as a certain amount of movement is made. Trailing stops can be great, but you're going to need a lot of optimization to really make them work, if you can pull it off at all.

Choosing Your Markets

It can be incredibly difficult figuring out just which markets to trade your system with. There are really only two ways to go about it. One way is to create a system, which can be traded in all markets. Your system's rules would remain the same, no matter what stock you choose. While the rules would remain the same, the parameters may or may not be touched up a bit.

The upside to applying this method to trading the markets is that there's more of a chance for great results. Your system is less susceptible to adverse market conditions as well, as it's been tested across all sorts of markets over time.

The drawback to this approach though, is it's going to make creating your system even more complicated. It's hard enough designing a strategy for one market. Add a bunch of other stocks, and you've got a lot of work ahead of you. One way to deal with this is to try out your strategy on all the stocks you'd like to trade, and then pick the best ones that work with your strategy. Do keep in mind though, that what you're really doing here is optimizing more than you have to, again.

The other way to pick your markets is to simply create a strategy, which fits the stock, or stocks you'll be trading. The great thing about this is you can make it fit the peculiar traits of each stock. If you've noticed the stocks you like to trade have a habit of always trending, you could take advantage of this by creating a trend following strategy, or a breakout strategy. For markets, which don't trend a lot, you might find more success using a mean reversion strategy. This approach of creating a strategy for a certain stock is definitely a lot easier than the multi-market approach. But what possible downside is there to this, if any?

When you create a strategy for each stock, you're assuming the stock will continue to be the same way, forever and ever, ad infinitum, ad nauseum. If there's one thing you should know about the markets — whatever markets you trade — they never, ever remain the same. So what happens when your trend following strategy stops working because the markets are suddenly choppy? How do you handle it when that relatively quiet stock suddenly decides it's a jolly good day to plummet to hell or shoot for the moon? Will your mean reversion strategy for that stock still work? Of course not.

I'm not really trying to make an argument for either one of these approaches. I'm simply pointing out the pros and cons of each market selection process. What you can do is have a mixture of both. It helps to have a bunch of strategies designed for a single market, and strategies, which apply, to multiple markets. Performances will vary, but you'll be increasing your odds of success doing it this way.

Type of Strategy

When you want to create your strategy, you need to figure out if it's going to be scalping, day trading, or swing trading. This automatically tells you what you need to do to make your algorithm works for you.

Homing in on day trading, there are a lot of benefits to this trading style. For starters, not only will you not have to pay swap fees, you're also protected from risky situations, which could happen overnight, since you generally have closed out your trades by the end of the session. It's also much easier to trade because you've got less in the way of margin requirements, so you can really go big with your position sizes — only if you've mastered your strategy down pat, of course. If you haven't this could be disastrous to your account and your confidence.

When you begin to develop your strategy, you could begin with the smallest of time frames, such as the 5 minute, or even the 1 minute. Unless you're proficient and fast, you might find these to be horrible for your account, and your psyche. So what do you do next? Consider going up several more time frames. Invariably, what you'll find is that what seemed to be a completely rubbish strategy is actually doing much better on the higher time frames. It goes without saying that once you stop playing around with the 1 minute and 5 minute timeframes, you're no longer in scalping territory, but are now day trading and/or swing trading.

Time Frames

Let me say this from the get go: the higher the time frame, the more profitable you'll be. Unless you're an experienced scalper with a trusted system that includes proper risk and money management. Other than having a high win rate, there are other factors, which will make you profitable. A scalper might have a high win rate, but the question becomes, what happens in terms of trading costs?

Let us assume you've created a strategy, which takes trades once after 20 candles close. If you trade based off the daily time frame that means you'll only trade once in a month. Assuming the trading costs of each trade for a single contract is $5 that means in a year, you will have spent only $60 on trade costs.

Now let's take that same strategy and apply that to a timeframe that's much lower. Let's say, the 1 minute time frame. This means in a day, there will be 86,400 1-minute candlesticks. Now let's assume you have an algo that trades nonstop. In a single day, you will have made approximately 4,000 trades. Multiply that by 5. I'll wait. Fine, you won't be in the market all day every day. You'll only keep your scalps to about 10 trades. Guess how much that is in a day? $50. How much is that in a week? A month? A year? Sure, maybe your strategy is really fire. But the moves are way too small on those 1-minute charts.

Another argument for trading off higher time frames is that there is a lot less noise in the market. You can't really see what the actual trend is. You don't know what's happening on a grander scale. That's how you go long at the very top of a move in the opposite direction, or take a short when the momentum downward has died out. I suppose if you're always experiencing this, you could make a strategy out of it by taking the opposite trades of whatever you're thinking. It's just much better to trade off the higher time frames.

When you trade on smaller time frames, it becomes more important than ever for you to perfect your entries and exits. If you miss your entry by as much as a tick or two, then a huge chunk of what would have been your profits is gone. When trading off the daily timeframe, you don't have to worry as much about missing a tick or two.

Another thing to keep in mind is most high frequency trading is carried out on those small time frames, by firms, which have all the resources to beat you at the game. They've got the speed, and they've got the precision. Think about that. On a higher time frame, they can't keep booting you out of your trade, because you're following the bigger picture, like a pro.

Finally, with most strategies, even the bad ones, you're better off trading less. On a lower time frame, there will be more signals generated. Most newbies erroneously assume more signals are better than not having enough, because it means more opportunities to make money. Make no mistake, money is made on the lower time frames. By your broker. From you. If you don't know what you're doing. I added that little caveat in, because there are extremely profitable strategies, which work on lower time frames, but if you want to play safe, don't go low. Stay high.

Your strategy's performance will depend on the time frames you choose. Therefore, it's important you select a frame of time, which will serve you best. If you've tried everything else, and you know you're a true scalper, then you might consider trading based on the 1 minute, or even using tick charts. Are you a swing trader? Then you might prefer to look at the dailies. If you're a day trader, you could use a 15 minute chart, or a 30 minute chart. Basically, choose a time frame, which matches your temperament.

If you're a scalper, then you need to find a broker which offers you tight spreads and minimal transaction costs, so you can truly enjoy your scalping — especially when you have a strategy that actually gives you impressive results.

To settle on a time frame, what you want to do is see how your strategy does on a specific time frame, and then adjust accordingly. Go up or down a few time frames to see what works best.

How to Program Your Strategy

When you have your essential entry and exit principles thoroughly thought out, you have chosen a market to trade, your preferred time period, the bar size you wish to test and all the historical data you need, then the time has come to assemble the pieces together, and put your strategy to the test. The question for a great many traders at this critical stage is, "would I be able to program the strategy myself?" The answer for a genuine DIY guy is a hundred percent "yes." But on the off chance that you have no idea how to do the programming using the software you have for running tests, this might be a scary task. But it doesn't have to be.

You could simply get an expert programmer to set up the strategy for you, especially if you have no interest in learning about programming — which, understandably, is quite a broad topic in its own right.

You could choose to either hire one expert, or you could hire an entire team and have them compartmentalized, so they don't all have a complete picture of your strategy. Do bear in mind that if you're going this route, it's going to cost you money and time, especially as you'll need to make adjustments and updates to the code along the way. You can find expert programmers on forums, or through your broker.

You might find it much better for you in the long run to simply team up with an expert in programming who will be interested in using the finished code to trade too. This way, they're not going to steal your original idea, and you can actually work on even more profitable trading systems as a team.

In the end though, there's nothing like doing it yourself. Whatever software packages you choose to go with will always have books, tutorials online, classes, and sample strategies, so you can learn how to code yourself. When you choose to program your strategy yourself, you can be at ease, because you never have to worry about anyone stealing your intellectual property. Also, as you become better and more familiar with the programming process, you'll inevitably understand what goes into the backtesting process as well. If you've been following this book so far, then you understand how valuable it is to deeply understand the backtesting process.

Chapter 10: All about Data

Data is easily one of the most ignored, yet supremely important aspects of testing out your strategy. You should never take data for granted, because it can come back to bite you in the you-know-where. Different sources of market data can yield remarkably different results from the very same strategy with the same parameters. This happens more often than you think!

It doesn't matter who your data vendor is; chances are that your market data will not be completely clean. There may be missing data, bad data points, and all other things that could go wrong with market data.

That said, you need to know the answers to a few key questions, when it comes to data. Just how much data will you be using to test your strategy? Will you make use of pit data, or choose electronic data instead? Are you going to use a continuous contract data? How has electronic trading affected market data, if at all it has? Let's dive deeper.

Data Needed

To make a proper test of your strategy, you need to have made enough trades, and tried out your strategy under a good number of market conditions. If you're going to do this, and be successful over the long haul, then you'll need lots more data. As much as you can possibly get.

The reason is simple. When you have more data, you have more to test your strategy against. You can figure out how well it does in bull markets, versus bear markets. You know what it's like in flat markets. You know how it fares during periods of high volatility, and low volatility as well. More data means you can be certain if your strategy continues to stay golden, then it's likely it will remain that way when you go live. More data means the success you have had in testing your strategy wasn't simply a fluke. More trades will give you more certainty that you've gone a winner — or a stinker — on your hands.

If you're trading a strategy based off of the daily time frame, you would be better off with at least 10 years' worth of data, so you know what your strategy is like in various market conditions, and see what would really need to be tweaked, if anything at all.

For the intraday trader, you could also opt for 10 years' worth of data — though it isn't always easy to obtain this much data. If you can get it, great! If not, then you should be looking for at least 5 years of data.

If you still cannot access as much as 5 years' worth of data, then you need to do the best with what you have. The next best thing in this scenario would be to place at least 30 trades to 100 trades with your strategy, for each rule and parameter you set up. For instance, if you have 3 entry rules, and 3 exit rules, then you want to have anywhere from 180 trades to 600 trades. You could choose lesser figures, but you might find yourself with curve fitted results.

Keep in mind, though, that the more data you use, the longer it will take to develop your system, and the tougher the process will be. It's best to think long term. In the end, it will be worth it to have created a system that can best any conditions thrown at it.

Pit, or Electric?

Way back in the day, it was just pit data. Now, there are several options. You could choose to run with pit data, or you could choose electronic data only. You could put the two together. You also have the option of using data from just the old-school pit times, or you could opt for data from all hours. You could choose data from day sessions, or from evening sessions alone.

When trading live, it only makes sense to focus on electronic data. This is where we're at right now. What happens though, when you want to test a strategy and you need to use two decades of data? I assure you that twenty years ago, all you had was pit data. So you obviously have to work with that.

Let's take gold as an example. In a pit trading session for the day, you'd most likely have anywhere from six to eight bars of 60 minutes each — considering that trading hours have been in a state of flux over the years. So if you made use of a 14 period exponential moving average, which would account for two days of trading. In today's markets though, that 14 period exponential moving average would only account for just about half of the trading day, rather than two days like it was 20 years ago. This is sure to have an impact on your historical testing.

The question becomes, what do you do with this data? You need to make the pit data and electronic data the same. You could simply select a time block, and make that your standard daily session time. Apply that block to the entire historical data. This way, you have data that won't screw up your test results.

Continuous Contracts

Most newbie traders are not quite sure what to do with continuous contracts when if comes to market testing. These contracts are actually quite necessary though, and that's because when you're trading stock futures, each contract has a very limited period of validity, while the continuous contracts give a ceaseless stream of data.

The best and most efficient method of testing with futures data, is to simply make use of the contract data as it is — raw. This way, you will not need to bother yourself so much about the continuous contracts. The unfortunate thing though, is that it's hard to find any trading software, which can make the process easy for you. With most software, you can only optimize on the data from one chart. Using multiple charts is impossible, unless you do so manually — and it's a walk in the park... if you were barefoot and the path was littered with broken class and sharp, yet rusty pieces of metal.

There are several ways for you to create a continuous contract — each one with their own pros and cons. You could have a 'non-adjusted continuous contract,' which would keep the original data intact, or you could use a 'back adjusted contract,' where all gaps are eliminated, and all the data is adjusted to match that.

Effects of the Electronic Markets

A lot of system developers only run their tests on electronic data, which means they only focus on the more recent years. There is the assumption that the advent of the electronic markets irrevocably changed the landscape of the markets for good, so whatever works fine now does not need to have worked just as well with the historical pit data. This is both true, and untrue.

The markets are different now. Pricing dynamics have changed, since pit trading was phased out. Most former pit traders who made a killing are not doing as well with electronic trading. The techniques used in pit trading days are not as profitable now as they were back then.

But when we pull back and really get a bird's eye view on things, all markets are affected by a law as old as mankind — supply and demand. This has always been the case, and will always be the case, whether you're trading on the pit floor, electronically, or psychically for that matter. It is illogical to assume that the high frequency trading firms which only hold positions for seconds at a time are the ones who ultimately dictate where price goes in the days, weeks, months, and even years to come.

That said, it would still be of great benefit to make use of historical data from the pit, when developing your strategy. If you can, that is. Not using pit data doesn't necessarily render your testing invalid.

Hopefully, you have an idea of just what the issues are when it comes to data. You need to understand the data you're using to test out your strategy. If you use the wrong data, or use the right data wrongly, you can get very inaccurate results from your tests — and the sad part is you might never even realize it. So do take the time out to properly go over the market data. It's matters just as much as your entries and exits do.

Chapter 11: Diversifying Your Systems

In the process of creating your trading system, you'll find that it would be best for you to diversify. You don't want to have all your eggs in one basket. That could work, but it would be best to simultaneously test a series of strategies, so you can make better use of your time and energy. This is because most of what you come up with will probably end up in the trash, so it's better to have several strategies you're working on, and not just one. Like it or not, trading systems can and do fail, even if they had proven profitable in the past. So why focus on one strategy? Diversification is your friend!

The Benefits of Diversification

For starters, you never have to worry about your systems if they disappoint you. You've got several more you're testing which should do better. If you trade just one system, what you'll find is that you don't really have a lot of options. Say the system works best with mean reversion. What happens when the stocks you've chosen to trade suddenly decide to trend strong and trend indefinitely? What do you do then? Leave trading? Chuck it in a bucket and call it quits? This is why it's best to have options.

Once you have various systems with various trading styles, you know you'll be able to make money in whatever market. The market really only ever does one of three things: trend up, trend down, or go sideways. So have systems in place, which can take advantage of these conditions.

Another advantage to using multiple trading systems, is you'll have less issues with fills. Here's the thing: as you trade your precious, single system, you're going to have growth in your equity. As your equity grows, you're going to increase the size of your positions. Sooner or later, your positions will be large enough to affect the prices you get filled at. You'll experience more slippage than usual. On the flip side, when you trade a variety of systems, then you've got smaller position sizes with each one. The result is that you don't have to worry about being filled at the worst possible prices.

Your equity curve will also gain a lot from you diversifying. How so? You've got a whole lot of variety going on. You've got various systems, timeframes, and markets, and all of these come together to help you get a smoother, better equity curve. Better than the kind those unscrupulous vendors try to sell you. The cumulative effect of all this variety includes less drawdown, and less susceptibility to adverse market conditions, which can develop, with no warning.
Now, we're going to take a look at the various ways you can measure diversification.

Daily Return Correlation

What you want to do when using this method is to use Excel to run a correlation analysis on the returns of each of your strategies, on a day to day basis. If you have a few systems, which are intraday, then you could run the same analysis, but just use shorter time periods — like the hourly time frame. Then you can check the correlation over the course of all the historical data you have, and then check again against a six month period to a full year. Get the results for your strategies, plotting one as X and the other as Y, then calculate the correlation coefficient of R^2. You want to aim for a lower correlation coefficient. If it's below 1.0, then you've got a really high diversification.

I must warn though, that this low, long term correlation doesn't mean there will never be times when your systems are correlated. In fact, for stretches of time, they could display high correlation. If you're an aggressive trader when it comes to the sizes of your positions, then you want to demonstrate extra care, as strategies have been known to suddenly develop a correlation to each other, which would further put you at risk. One time markets suddenly became correlated was back in 2008, with the financial crisis.

Equity Curve Linearity

The best curve for your trading system to have is a flawless, linear one. This is also a good measure of diversification. How? Run a linear regression on the equity curve of your strategy in Excel, and then get the value of the correlation coefficient R^2. The best value to get would be 1, which would show that perfect linear equity curve.

You might find that the R^2 value for the aggregate of systems is better than that of each individual system. This is another argument for diversification.

Max Drawdown

Yet another way to calculate the effect of diversification. A caveat: using a variety of trading systems does not necessarily mean drawdown will be reduced, but more often than not, it does help. It's not hard to check this, once you've for the equity curve for each system, and that for the combination of systems.

Monte Carlo Analysis

You can use the Monte Carlo analysis to see if the aggregate of systems performs much better when adjusted for risk. What you need to do is take the yearly percentage return, and divide that by the max percentage drawdown. If you get high values that means you're getting more rewards than what you're risking.

Using an aggregate of systems usually leads to a much smoother equity curve. You'll have less drawdown than the worst of the systems on its own. You'll also enjoy a much better risk-reward ratio, and have a higher likelihood of making returns. Diversification is how you make each system even better than it would be on its own.

You don't need to be a mathematical wiz to diversify. You just need to make your strategies as different as night and day, use a variety of entry and exit parameters, and it just happens. This is quite simple and to the point.

In the end, you'll find that diversification helps you make your good systems even better — together. So you can be a bit more at ease regarding your performance targets, as diversification will naturally improve it. You might find that your strength isn't in creating the strategy to end all strategies, but in creating a bunch of fairly decent strategies, which together become an unstoppable force. This means, in the end, you'll be that much closer to your ultimate goal — making enough money to buy your own private island.

Chapter 12: Money Management

Position sizing is one of the most critical elements of successful trading. This doesn't mean it's the only thing you should focus on, like most people would have you believe. You could have the best positions sizes, and still wipe your account away with the worst strategy in the long run.

There Is No Best Way to Size Positions

This is the way I see it. There's no right way or wrong way to size your positions. Sure, you may have read a book or two which claim they've got the holy grail of position sizing, and they'll show you a couple of examples, but in the end, it's all hogwash. It's not hard to find the best position sizing model, which will fit perfectly well with a certain equity curve. To suggest that that's the best way to size your positions is inaccurate though. A position sizing method, which works great with one trading system, will not necessarily work well with others.

Risk and Reward — An Inseparable Pair

Yet another unrealistic search, is for position sizing methods, which will offer even more rewards, with no added risk. Risk and rewards actually work in tandem. Want more rewards? Then you'll need to risk more. That's the way it goes. Sure, you could find a position sizing method that seems to have achieved this — judging from the equity curve. But the fact is there's always risk. The risk and drawdown may not have shown on the equity curve, but it's there. It's always there — it's just not realized. So always assume that more rewards means more risk. Make peace with that.

Optimizing Position Sizes

Some traders work on creating a strategy, and take it through all the hoops. Then they'll check out all sorts of position sizing methodologies, and select what they feel is the best one. In other words, what they have basically done is optimize the position size. Remember, we've always said just because it worked in the past, does not mean it will work in future trades. If you must set out on this path, then perhaps you would be better off running your methods through the Monte Carlo analysis, which will let you know what position sizes are best to use — if there's any method in particular which trumps the rest to begin with.

You Can't Make a Loser Win

It doesn't matter what sort of position sizing technique you use, if your strategy sucks, you **will** lose. Trust me on that. There is no magic formula of sizing your positions, which would save you. It just won't happen! If you're going to succeed at trading, you need an edge. You need a solid strategy, which you've tested, backtested, and analyzed properly, which shows you would indeed be profitable when you go live with it. Size doesn't matter if you have no edge.

You Can Have a Winner Lose

It would make sense logically that if a losing system cannot be turned into a winning one, then a winning one cannot be made into a losing one, right? Well this is not the case. You can have winning trading systems, which become losers over time. Remember, the market is always in a state of flux. What trends today may range tomorrow, and vice versa. About the only thing that could help you out here is diversification. So just because you've got some award-winning position sizing technique with a stellar trading system does not guarantee you will not blow your account. So don't be too aggressive. Else, you're going to crash and burn.

Don't Believe the Hype

You may have had some system vendors tell you that they can guarantee you a profit of $10,000 for each contract, each year. Then they'll ask you to envision the possibilities... What if you traded 10 contracts? 100? 1,000? You could buy your own country! Hopefully you now know not to believe the hype. First of all, you need to have enough money to be able to trade 100 contracts, which, let's face it, you probably don't. So don't listen to the scammers. Listen to your account. Another thing is there's always the chance of drawdown. Do you have enough to handle it? Consider that, while they try to sell you on their BS. Another thing is that not everyone can handle 100 contracts well, from a psychological point of view. How do I know this? You can imagine trading that and winning. Sounds like a nice, easy half a mill in the bank for the year. Now imagine trading 100 contracts and losing. 6 times in a row. Ah. There you go.

Short Term Winnings

When you have an edge that isn't all that impressive, and you're only interested in trading for the short term, then you can go nuts with the sizes of your position. In the short run, you could get away with this. Over the long term though, it's going to kill you. One example is trading with the Martingale strategy. Each time you register a loss, you double your bet next time. And the next, and then the next, until you make back all you lost, plus a little extra. You may make some winnings in the short term, but sooner or later, your odds will drop dramatically to zero. Why? There will be a long string of losses that you will not recover from, unless you've got ridiculously deep pockets. You could win a sequence, but chances are you'll lose the next. It takes some serious discipline for people to know when to fold 'em and run. Serious discipline most people lack.

When Size Matters

You could have a winning trading system, but if you don't adjust your trading size over the years, then it's almost just as nuts as going in with ridiculously huge position sizes. When you've got the cow, you milk it. Make the most of it if you have a system that guarantees you win after win while it works!

Strategize, Then Position Size

When you are developing your system, the first thing to work on should be the system itself. You would also be doing yourself a huge favor if you kept it to just one contract. Once you're done developing your system, and you're sure that it works, then the next thing you can work on is developing your position sizing technique. This is the best way to do it, especially when you're working with a diversification of trading systems.

However, don't take my word for it. The thing about trading is that there are as many ways to go about it as there are traders. It's like life. There are many ways to live it — some being more fulfilling than others. A few other professional traders actually take a stance opposite to mine; the argument being that factoring in the size of positions along size the system development process helps make sure there are less losing trades. This in turn will allow you to trade with more contracts, and in the end, you'll have much higher returns. I must confess it does make sense. I will not be so arrogant as to insist that it's my way or the highway.

Trade Small

When you begin trading a new strategy, it would be best to start with the smallest sizes possible. No more than just a contract. However, most people do the exact opposite. They want to go big right from the get go. They believe if you've got a great edge, then you need to exploit the heck out of it. There's a chance that edge might disappear, so why not make the most of it? I agree. This is valid. But I've learned over the years that it is far wiser — and better for your account — to start small. It's quite possible the edge you perceive is present isn't actually there. So what you can do is just trade small until you're sure, without a shred of doubt that you're onto something.

Another reason to trade small in the beginning is on account of emotions. Sure, you're trading with algos, so you don't have to get involved more than necessary, but what happens when you program in a **really large** amount of contracts, and you watch just a tiny bit of drawdown which looks like it's about to get you a margin call from your broker? What then? Can you actually sit on your hands and do nothing, without worsening an already terrible situation? Do you now understand it's better to trade small in the beginning? Drawdown of 10 ticks with just a contract is a much easier thing to handle, than drawdown of 3 ticks with 200 contracts. Think about that.

Finally, you want to increase the size of your account not by overleveraging and really bad money management, **but on account of your edge.** If you really do have a good edge, then you never have to worry about whether or not you will make money in the long run, because I promise you, you will. Your account will blossom. If however, your strategy loses money, then at least you can rest easy knowing you still have more than enough to come back and play another day.

You could make use of fractional sizing. How does that work? Here's the formula:

$N = int (x * Equity/Largest Loss)$

Where

N	=	Rounded down integer number of contracts
Int	=	Function of Integer
X	=	Risked fraction of equity per trade
Equity	=	Account equity as at present

Largest Loss = Largest recorded loss historically, from walk forward backtest

The one variable thing is the fixed fraction. Some traders will insist that x needs to be .02 or less, or some random value. There's nothing wrong with keeping x low, but I've found that the Monte Carlo simulation is the best way to determine what would be the best value of x, in order to help me have a better risk to reward ratio. I use this, keeping in mind that there are a few other things to keep watch on, such as my max permissible drawdown, and the risk of ruin.

Multi-System Position Sizing

When trading multiple positions at a time, it's important to pay attention to whatever correlation there might be across the results. You can't just look at the results for each system individually, and then trade them together. What you should do is analyze the systems as an aggregate, and then you can attempt all the values of x for each one. What you're looking for, ideally, is a value of x, which proves to be of benefit to your risk to reward and reward to drawdown ratios. while also considering the maximum permissible drawdown and the risk of ruin as well.

It should be obvious to you that we've only just touched the tip of the iceberg when it comes to position sizing. There is a whole lot more that goes into this, and you can read and research further in order to learn more. But the basic thing you need to recall when sizing your positions is to start nice and slow. Let your system be the reason you make profits — not your insane overleveraging. You might choose to go a different route than fractional sizing. The choice really is up to you. You can take all you have learned here, and put your own spin on things. Be sure to conduct a proper analysis, so you know whether or not your take is actually better for you.

Chapter 13: Documentation

You've probably already figured out that it can be quite tedious keeping tabs on the strategies you've created. It's absolutely essential, however, that you keep some records. When you document your work, you're better able to handle your strategies and manage them effectively. So what is it that's worth tracking, as you develop your algo trading systems?

Your Trading Goals

You need to have goals. We've already covered that. You need to also make sure each goal is clearly documented. What profits would you like to have? What's the drawdown you want to deal with? What about your return rates? How many trades per day or session? These, among others, should be noted down. In the long run, it will help you weed out systems, which do not match up to these goals, since they're boldly written where you can see them.

Your Algo Trading System Idea

You want to make sure you write down the name of your strategies — so you can tell them apart from each other easier, and you can keep better track of results. Also, you'll find it easier to keep track of different versions of a strategy. For instance, if you have a strategy you name 'The Rainbow,' you might have a version of it called 'The Rainbow 2.0' or 'The Rainbow A.' Whatever floats your boat. This is a great way to know how many updates you've made to each strategy over time, so you know when it's time to call it quits if 'The Rainbow' has hit version 666 and it's time to send it to hell and move on. You can also add initials to signal what phase of the testing you're at with each strategy.

Another thing to note is the description of your strategy. Next, note down the edge of your strategies. If you have no idea what your strategies edges are, then chances are they don't exist, and you need to work on better ones.

Write down the stocks you plan to test your strategies on. Also note down the bar size r time frame, as well as the block of time you'll be doing the testing on, historically. Another thing to note are the streams you'll be using for the market data, and any customization on session times which you may have created.

Finally, you need to note down your entry and exit rules. Describe them in plain English, or in pseudo code, or if you're familiar with actually code, then use that instead.

Limited Testing

Here, you'll note all the details pertaining to the test period, and the sample of historical data you're using to perform your limited testing. You'll also record the results you've got from testing your entries, whether good, bad, or average. Same thing with exits as well.

When you run a test on your algo system's core, you want to note the results of the entire system. If you made use of monkey testing (testing random inputs) then you definitely want to note down the results you go as well.

Finally, note down the overall result of your limited testing on your system. Was it a pass? Was it a fail? Document it.

Walk Forward Testing

Here, you need to note down how many days were in the in-sample periods, as well as the out-sample periods. Note down the fitness function you made use of, and whether or not you used anchored or unanchored testing. Any optimization of the in-periods and out-periods should also be noted down. If you wound up with a better version of your strategy in the process of testing, write that down as well. Finally, note whether or not your system was a hit or a miss after the testing.

Monte Carlo Testing

If your strategy passed the walk forward testing, then it's time for the Monte Carlo analysis. So what you'll document here will include the initial equity, before you began your simulation runs, the quit equity, which is the level at which you will give up on the strategy, the amount of trades taken in a year, the return rate and the draw down ratio, and finally, the end results of the Monte Carlo testing — hit, or miss.

Incubation Testing

When your strategy has passed the Monte Carlo analysis, then you can move on to documenting the incubation testing. Did it meet your goals? Did it pass or fail? Document the results.

Diversification Testing

If you're trading an aggregate of systems, then you want to note down whether or not the strategy was created with the goal of diversification. Did it meet your goals?

Position Sizing Analysis

If you only trade one contract per trade, then this is easy to check and document. If you used some fancy position sizing though, then you should note it down at this point, especially when it's traded as part of an aggregate of systems.

Did it meet your goals? Did you create the strategy to work with just one contract for each trade, or did you use some other position sizing technique, which doesn't include the optimization process?

Final Observations

Once you're through with testing and developing your algo trading strategy, then you need to add in any other information that you might deem important. You could note down when you began trading the strategy. You could write down your sentiments — for instance, the strategy may not have passed all your testing, but you may have liked the entry rules, or the exit rules, or both. If that's the case, document your thoughts, because you'll be glad you did later, when working on other systems. You could take elements of a failed system and apply them to other stocks, and you'd find yourself thrilled with the results.

The great thing about documentation is how it makes it so much easier to manage your strategies. You can also keep other lists that are important, besides what I've mentioned here. You might have a bunch of ideas for entries and exits, which are not fully fleshed out as yet, but can also be tested. Rather than make a mental note, you can write it down as well.

I always make a habit of noting down ideas and whatever flashes of inspiration I might have. Time and time again, it helps me with creating new strategies, and it never hurts to always have new things to test out. Remember, a few of these ideas may have more to them that meets the eye. So document it all!

Conclusion

Now we've finally come to the end of this book! I want to believe you know all you need to know now, to set off on your journey in developing successful algos for trading. This book is by no means the be all and end all of it. There is so much more for me to share. There is lots more for you to explore. But I'm choosing to believe I've at least helped you get off on the right foot.

Before we round up completely, I just want to share a few more thoughts. First of all, trading is not easy. Don't let anyone tell you it is, because it really isn't. It's tough. Those who dabble in trading for fun are trading against actually pros that have been at this for years. They know how to take your money, and if you don't prepare adequately before you go live, they will. Know that. I don't mean to scare you, but it is what it is.

There's no such thing as a holy grail. If anyone comes up to you and says they've got it, you pick up your legs, and run. Run hard, and run fast. There is no magical strategy that can accurately call tops and bottoms one hundred percent of the time. It's not possible, and it doesn't exist. There is no such thing as a completely risk free strategy either. You're a trader. You need to learn to make friends with risk. This is risky business, but done right, the rewards are well worth it, and you will reap it.

The way to make your way to being one of the top dogs in trading, is by finding your own way. You need to invest the time in creating your own strategy. You need to put in the work. Commit to it. The process is neither pretty nor easy. You will lose money. You will find yourself wondering why the heck you got into this on occasion. But I promise you, if you stick with it, and you do what you need to do, versus try to skirt around the necessary steps, slowly but surely, you'll make some progress.

Remember, there is no strategy, which works forever and always. So don't be afraid to keep inventing. Keep testing. Keep trying out every idea you get — no matter how silly. Don't listen to the peanut gallery. Keep testing!

Keep in mind that you could have the best trading psychology in the world, but if your strategy is not profitable, if it has no edge, then you will not make any money. I don't care if you meditate so hard you leave your body before you begin each trading session. You need an edge. This is why you need to create your strategies, and test the heck out of them.

It's going to take a lot of work. I can't stress this enough. I've documented all my testing over the years, and I found I've tested hundreds and hundreds of ideas. Most people who aren't really in this 100% would have quit way before then. Don't be most people. Not if you really want to succeed. Keep at it!

Don't forget to set your goals. One thing I have learned over the years is to 'set small goals, then crush them.' Trust me when I say it's important to set goals. When you've got a goal, it becomes easy for your mind to zero in on what's really needed to make your trading take off! I've already mentioned the goals you need to set when it comes to your algo trading system. But there's another goal that is just as important. Set a financial goal. I know it seems a bit of a cliché, but you need to know where you're going — otherwise, how will you know when you've gotten there? Know how much it is you want to make in a year. Know when you'd like that to become a reality for you. This way, you're that much closer to making it happen.

Stay flexible, and stay open. There will be times when you want to stubbornly hold on to an idea you have romanticized. You believe with all of your heart that this should work! There's no reason for it not to! While it's great to have a persevering spirit, know when it is okay to let go. Know when you truly have done your best, and it's time to find some other way around the problem you're facing with your strategies. I promise you, the solution is always there, but you need to be ready, and stay open. You'll spot it.

As much as you can, work with others. Others who are as skilled as you are, or better than you are. Together, you'll come up with ideas, which can prove wildly profitable! There's truth in the saying 'two heads are better than one.' There is power in synergy, and you'll get there twice as fast.

I wish you the best of luck, and I wish you the best of trades!

References

Arnuk, Sal L., and Joseph C. Saluzzi. Broken Markets: How High Frequency Trading and Predatory Practices on Wall Street Are Destroying Investor Confidence and Your Portfolio. Upper Saddle River, NJ: FT Press, 2012.

Beckert, Walter. Course notes on Financial Econometrics, Birkbeck University of London, 2011. Available at www.ems.bbk.ac.uk/for_students/bsc_FinEcon/fi n_economEMEC007U/adf.pdf.

Bernard, Victor L., and Jacob K. Thomas. "Post-Earnings-Announcement Drift: Delayed Price Response or Risk Premium?" Journal of Accounting Research 27 (1989): 1–36.

Berntson, M. "Steps in Significance/Hypothesis Testing Using the Normal Distribution." Course notes for Introduction to Sociology, Grinnell College, 2002. Available at http://web.grinnell.edu/courses/sst/s02/sst115-03/practice/hypothesisteststeps1.pdf.

Bollen, Johan, Huina Mao, and Xiao-Jun Zeng. "Twitter Mood Predicts the Stock Market," 2010. Available at http://arxiv.org/pdf/1010.3003.pdf.

Bryant, Martin. "Investment Fund Set to Use Twitter to Judge Emotion in the Market," The Next Web, December 16, 2010. Available at http://thenextweb.com/uk/2010/12/16/investment-fund-set-to-use-twitter-to-judge-emotion-in-the-market/

Buy the Hype, "The 'Twitter Hedge Fund' Has an Out-of-Sample Experience," Buy the Hype (blog), May 3, 2012. Available at http://sellthenews.tumblr.com/post/22334483882/derwents-performance.

Chan, Ernest. Quantitative Trading: How to Build Your Own Algorithmic Trading Business. Hoboken, NJ: John Wiley & Sons,

Daniel, Ken, and Tobias Moskowitz. "Momentum Crashes." Preprint, 2011. Available at www.columbia.edu/~kd2371/papers/unpublished/mom4.pdf.

Dever, Michael. Jackass Investing. Thornton, PA: Ignite LLC, 2011.

Fama, Eugene F., and Marshall E. Blume. "Filter Rules and Stock-Market Trading." Journal of Business 39, no. 1 (1966): 226–231. Available at www.e-m-h.org/FaBl66.pdf.

Friedman, Thomas. "A Good Question." New York Times Op-ed, February 25, 2012.

Gill, Jeff. "The Insignificance of Null Hypothesis Significance Testing." Political Research Quarterly 52, no. 3 (1999): 647–674. Available at www.artsci.wustl.edu/~jgill/papers/hypo.pdf.

Greenblatt, Joel. The Little Book that Beats the Market. Hoboken, NJ: John Wiley & Sons, 2006. Also see magicformulainvesting.com.

Hafez, Peter A. "Event Trading Using Market Response," July 22, 2011, www.ravenpack.com/research/marketresponsepaperform.htm.

Hafez, Peter A., and Junqiang Xie. "Short-Term Stock Selection Using News Based Indicators," May 15, 2012, www.ravenpack.com/research/shorttermstockselectionpaperform.htm.

Malkiel, Burton. A Random Walk Down Wall Street: The Time-Tested Strategy for Successful Investing. New York: W. W. Norton, 2008.

Osler, Carol. "Support for Resistance: Technical Analysis and Intraday Exchange Rates." Federal Reserve Bank of New York Economic Policy Review 6 (July 2000): 53–65.

Patterson, Scott. The Quants. New York: Crown Business, 2010.

Philips, Matthew. "Unlocking the Crude Oil Bottleneck at Cushing."

Bloomberg BusinessWeek, May 16, 2012. Available at www.businessweek.com/articles/2012-05-16/unlocking-the-crude-oil-bottleneck-atcushing#p1.

Serge, Andrew. "Where Have All the Stat Arb Profits Gone?" Columbia University Financial Engineering Practitioners Seminars, January 2008.

Simon, David P., and Jim Campasano. "The VIX Futures Basis: Evidence and Trading Strategies," 2012. Available at SSRN: http://papers.ssrn.com/sol3/papers.cfm?abstract_id=2094510.

Sinclair, Euan. Option Trading: Pricing and Volatility Strategies and Techniques. Hoboken, NJ: John Wiley & Sons, 2010.

www.ingramcontent.com/pod-product-compliance
Lightning Source LLC
Chambersburg PA
CBHW062110220526
45471CB00010B/3683